Nannies, Maids & More

The Complete Guide for Hiring Household Help

Copyright © 1989, by Linda F. Radke, Scottsdale, AZ
All rights reserved. No part of this book may be reproduced, stored in a retrieval system or transcribed in any means, electronic, mechanical, photocopying, recording or otherwise, without the written permission of the publisher. For information write to: Five Star Publications, P.O. Box 3142, Scottsdale, AZ 85271-3142.

"This publication is designed to provide accurate and authoritative information in regard to the subject matter covered. It is sold with the understanding that the publisher is not engaged in rendering legal, accounting, or other professional service."

From a Declaration jointly adopted by a
Committee of the American Bar Association
and a Committee of Publishers.

ISBN 0-9619853-2-1
Library of Congress Catalog Number: 89-80249

Edited by: Mary E. Hawkins
Drawing of my father by: Michael J. Woodruff
Book illustrations by: Pat Flanigan
Cover design by: Christine Barringer

Printed in the United States of America

Nannies, Maids & More

The Complete Guide for Hiring Household Help

DEDICATION

Marvin B. Foster
February 27, 1921 – September 21, 1988

Dad if you're listening...
I hope you can hear...
the love you gave is so close and so near...

Dad, to you I dedicate this book.
To the person who showed me courage and left me with strength.

SPECIAL THANKS ARE DUE TO.....

My friend Diane Berger, whose banana bread kept me alive during the initial stages of writing this book.

My mother whose banana cream pie lured me back to the manuscript at the wee hours of the night.

Dorothy Tegeler for her encouragement of my writing this book. A little encouragement can go a long way.

Mary Westheimer of Arizona Authors' Association for being there and providing invaluable information in getting this book together.

Mary E. Hawkins for editing.

Christine Barringer for designing the cover.

Michael J. Woodruff for doing a superb drawing of my father.

Pat Flanigan for doing a great job on the illustrations.

Mary Gilmore of GraphicWorks for her fine work and patience in typesetting *Nannies, Maids & More.*

Janet Fullerton, an Acquisitions and Collection Development Librarian with Mesa Public Library, for taking the time to review *Nannies, Maids & More.*

My husband, Lowell, for seeing me through this and so much more.

CONTENTS

Dedication		v
Special Thanks		vii
PROLOGUE	Hiring on your own	1
CHAPTER 1	I need help…human help	5
CHAPTER 2	I want someone to stay forever	9
CHAPTER 3	How long does it take to find someone?	23
CHAPTER 4	How do I know I've got the right person?	39
CHAPTER 5	I've got someone, but I want to let her (or him) go	61
CHAPTER 6	I want to use an agency	69
CHAPTER 7	I want to use outside care	87
CHAPTER 8	Sample forms	95
EPILOGUE	The Test	109

PROLOGUE

Hiring on Your Own

The nature of hiring household help is a delicate one and needs to be handled as such. First impressions and gut level feelings can no longer be trusted. There is too much at stake—your loved ones. Some mistakes you can't afford to make twice, and shouldn't happen even once. Hiring the wrong sitter, for instance, may lead to disastrous results.

All too often, headlines read, "Sitter kidnaps baby," "Sitter harms baby," "Housekeeper wipes out household possessions." The frightening reality is that even with careful screening and the following of techniques suggested in this guide, you cannot be guaranteed that those things will not happen. But the odds are not nearly as likely if careful precautions are followed each time you hire someone.

And now for *Nannies, Maids & More...The Complete Guide for Hiring Household Help* (or do you really have what it takes to be an employer of household help?) After reading the text, take the test at the end of this book and determine if you have what it takes.

Finding the right employee is only the first step. Keeping that employee is the last. This book helps provide you with all the necessary "tools" and information that will help you avoid some of the common pitfalls when hiring. Choosing intelligently the first time will save you valuable time, energy, and money. And with the employee's viewpoint in mind, you can keep your household help productive, happy and working for you.

The predecessor to *Nannies, Maids & More* was published in 1985 as the *Domestic Screening Kit*. This

Prologue

updated, revised book form incorporates further insights gained from experience as the owner of a domestic employment agency, screening and interviewing close to five thousand candidates applying for household jobs.

Many a nanny, sitter, mother's helper, senior caretaker, couple, party server, gardener, and more were placed by using the techniques described here. If this book saves you time, money, and energy in training a new person, then it well serves its purpose.

1

I need help... human help

Suddenly, or perhaps not so suddenly, you realize that you need help in your household. Perhaps you have had someone before, and it hasn't worked out, or perhaps there is a new situation in your household. A new infant, an invalid or elderly relative to be cared for, a larger house, new social obligations, a full-time job or new responsibilities for you outside the home, or a dozen other changes may demand more human input than you now have available. There comes a time when all the organization in the world and all the technological helpers just aren't enough.

Don't panic.

Once you face up to the need and decide to try to do something about it, you're halfway there. Analyze the problem and determine exactly what kind of help you need and what routes you can take to locate the right person or persons.

One route is to act on your own. That is, you try to find someone by either inquiring among your friends or through advertising.

Another option is to work with a household employment agency.

For some types of positions—yard or pool care or heavy cleaning, for example—you may deal with a contractor who provides the service.

For some types of child care or care of a handicapped or elderly person, you may be able to gain the help you need by taking the child or other person to a day-care center.

The following chapters consider these alternatives and explain what to expect from each and how you can make the best use of each source.

2

I want someone to stay forever...

But how close can you come to "forever"?

How often I heard that as requests poured in for sitters. At the agency, I would explain my fee and the guarantees that came with it. My placement fee came with a 90-day guarantee. I soon discovered that clients would expect so much and offer so little. Many would expect child care, cleaning, cooking, running errands and…, and then offer $4 per hour. For my fee and the hourly wage the client wanted a guarantee that this person would stay with them "forever."

I soon learned that for $4 to $5 per hour, no one is going to stay forever. Would you? I found that with fair salary offers a client was lucky to have a worker remain on the job for a year. Consider anything beyond a year a bonus and a gift from heaven.

I recall one client who called after four years. I feared the worst, for she was in tears. The problem, after four years of employment was that the worker was quitting. If the client only knew how good she had had it.

What most affects the length of stay?

SALARIES: What to pay? If you can afford the luxury of household help, then pay what is fair. Time and again, I would hear clients brag about low salaries paid to household help. It wasn't as if they couldn't afford the help. Especially this came from people hiring live-in help.

I want someone to stay forever...

My advice is: Pay at least the going rate. You can find out the going rate for household help in your area by contacting the Department of Economic Security (or whatever the comparable agency is called in your area) or different household or nanny employment agencies. Look in your telephone book under such headings as: Sitting Services, Child Care, Senior Citizen Organizations, Employment Agencies. Call and ask their rates. Remember that even the best paid jobs don't guarantee longevity. However I did discover that the better paying jobs attracted a multitude of excellent candidates for our clients to interview.

I recall that one client offered a nanny/housekeeper $500 per week, plus benefits. The candidate had to be willing to care for two boys, clean the home, shift the care to the mother's home when the mother had the children and to the father's home when he was in charge. The candidate also had to be willing to fly in a small privately owned plane. It didn't take much advertising to attract a locally trained nanny.

"Locally trained" reminds me to warn you about hiring persons new to your area. One of the complaints coming from people living in Arizona, for example, is the extreme summer heat. The agency would get an influx of candidates during the winter

months. Life is wonderful, and temperatures remain warm and inviting…until May hits. The help stay until June, and then they are gone. Hiring those who are accustomed to your climate gives you better odds of their staying.

Another concern is social life. Do the employees have friends and family in your area? Some employers like to hire newcomers because they feel that the worker will be more dedicated to them and less interested in socializing. Others prefer their workers to have a life of their own and not depend on the family for social activities. All of which is saying: *Look at hiring from every angle.*

HOURS: After salaries, hours come in for a big share in misunderstanding and difficulty. Are you overworking someone? Some people overwork, while others underemploy, their household helpers. If you are hiring live-in workers, remember that they, just like you, want to have two days off a week. If that is not possible, then they deserve extra compensation. In the everyday work world, it is called overtime. It is amazing how the same people who fight for their rights in the work force, jump to the other side and fight the same issues tooth and nail with their household help.

Keep one thing in mind when offering a salary, benefits, and work schedule: Ask no more of the employee than you would be willing for an employer to ask of you. If you are only in need of a part-time worker, you will either need to compensate with a higher hourly wage or stretch the job in order to offer more hours. Not too many workers are willing to take a part-time job that offers less than twenty hours a week. If so, how long do you think they are likely to stay? Not too long is generally the case. Even grandmothers in search of part-time work, want something worth their efforts. For less than twenty hours, transportation costs and time are too great.

CONDITIONS OF EMPLOYMENT: This is an area which you must look at as critically and analytically as possible. Do you offer a pleasant work environment? Can any family frictions be hidden? At the agency, we soon found that some clients experiencing marital problems had a harder time keeping household help (no matter how good the salary). No one likes to witness personality clashes or work in an atmosphere of hostility, even if it isn't directed at the worker.

THE HUMAN TOUCH: Employees are not machines. They are human beings and respond to basic aspects of good interpersonal relationships. Here are a few to recognize and practice.

RESPECT: Often employees would come into our agency wanting a job change just because their current employer gave them no respect. Simple as it sounds, that touch was often missing.

PRAISE: Praise for a job well done was also often lacking. We all like to know, and be told, when we are doing a good job. The time taken to thank someone may leave you with one happy employee and with one less headache of having to rehire.

COMMUNICATION: All too often clients would come to me in need of a replacement. Why? They weren't happy with their current help. When asked why, I was told that the employees weren't doing the job that needed being done. When I asked if the employer had informed the workers of this, in nine out of ten times the answer was no. So many people are afraid to talk to each other. I found this to be true, even as an employer in my own office. Why is it so difficult to let someone know that he or she is not doing what needs to be done? Often, when clients would go home and communicate their needs to their help, the differences were soon ironed out, and the household was back to running smoothly and efficiently.

I had one particular client who hired a mother's helper. The job involved some cleaning, child care, and traveling with the family. The worker was paid $7.50 per hour. They were an ideal family to work for. They had a fabulous home, where love was felt and warmth was given to family members and nanny alike. The client originally hired one of our workers and was delighted with her. After being employed for nearly a year and a half, the worker had her own baby and gave up the job. The client was sad to let her go. She often told me that at night her children would call out for the nanny, not her.

When this client hired a new person, she knew it would be a difficult role for the new person to replace the well-loved previous nanny. No two people are alike. After a month or so, the client called me and wanted a replacement. When asked why, she replied that the new person didn't clean all the same places that the other one did. I asked her if she talked to her employee about this. She said no. Of course, after she confronted the new employee with what was on her mind, all things were settled.

We all need to be given a chance, especially those who come in as a replacement.

DISCIPLINE: If you are hiring a child or senior care provider, you need to discuss discipline philosophies. This person you are hiring will be taking over a major role in your household. During the interview, discuss discipline tactics to be used.

One of the sitters I placed, called me soon afterward and was very frustrated in not knowing what to do. She was a live-in sitter. The mother was a single parent. The mother would come home, and when the children misbehaved, the sitter did not know what to do. Sometimes she would discipline in front of the mother, and at other times she didn't. She felt awkward in both settings. I asked her to discuss with her employer about who was to discipline when the parent was at home. This way, if the parent feels most comfortable doing the disciplining when she is at home, the sitter does not feel that she is either a.) not doing her job or b.) intruding in the mother's territory. This is a prime example of what needs to be discussed during the initial interview, and later if the need arises.

PRIVACY: A big issue for both employers and

I want someone to stay forever…

employees. If you are in need of live-ins, you may fear a total loss of privacy. Take this up during the interview. Be up front; discuss your concerns when you are interviewing. It is easier at that meeting than when difficulties begin. You can avoid many of the common pitfalls by interviewing right the first time. When we screened for families wanting privacy, we made it clear that the family liked their privacy. For weekends, workers were asked not to enter the employer's home, just as the employer would not enter their living quarters. This, of course, applied to employers providing separate live-in quarters.

It is clear then, that if you want someone to stay "forever," it rests with you to *establish an environment of teamwork, mutual respect, liking, and dignity.* And, of course, to try to find employees who will respond in kind, for human relationships work both ways.

Laws governing the hiring of household help

As an employer, you will have to comply with certain laws. One of the newest is the Immigration

Reform and Control Act of 1986, which says that you should hire only American citizens and aliens who are authorized to work in the United States. You, the employer, will need to verify employment eligibility of anyone hired after November 6, 1986, by completing and retaining **Form I-9, Employment Eligibility Verification.**

A sample copy of Form I-9 is shown on page 96.

Write for:
    Handbook for Employers
    Instructions for Completing Form I-9
    U.S. Department of Justice
    Immigration and Naturalization Service
    425 I Street
    Washington, DC 20536

It includes copies of Form I-9, instuctions and explanations, and addresses for further information in each state, and a toll-free number (1-800-777-7700) for further information.

A long-standing requirement is, of course, that you and the employee must pay Social Security taxes if you pay the employee more than $50 in any calendar quarter. The present rate is 7.5% of the earnings (up to $48,000 per year).

To report the Social Security taxes and the wages paid, use:
> **IRS Form 942**
> Internal Revenue Service
> Department of the Treasury
> 1500 Pennsylvania Avenue, NW
> Washington, DC 20220

You will also need to provide each employee with an **IRS Form W-2 (Wage and Tax Statement)** by January 31 for the previous year. The IRS will usually send this form by the end of the year, or you may obtain the form from any IRS office.

You may also have to pay federal unemployment tax, which is your employee's unemployment insurance. See **Form 926, Employment Taxes for Household Employees** available from the IRS or from the Forms Distribution Center for your state.

Another federal statute that can apply to domestic service workers as well as to other workers is the Fair Labor Standards Act. Obtain a copy of: **How the Fair Labor Standards Act Applies to Domestic Service Workers, WH Publication 1382, Rev. March 1979.**

This publication is available from:
U. S. Department of Labor
Employment Standards Administration
Wage and Hour Division
200 Constitution Avenue, NW
Washington, DC 20210

It is also for sale by the Superintendent of Documents, U.S. Government Printing Office, Washington, DC 20402 (Stock No. 029-000-00368-8).

This publication clearly defines domestic service employees, conditions of the Act, rates of pay (minimum wage $3.35 an hour beginning January 1, 1981), and so forth.

The following records must be kept for three years (though no particular form is required):

- Name and Social Security number
- Address in full, including zip code
- Total hours worked each week for the employee
- Total cash wages paid each week to the employee by the employer

- Weekly sums claimed by the employer for board, lodging, or other facilities
- Extra pay for weekly hours in excess of 40 by the employee for the employer.

3

How long does it take to find someone...
How do I do it?

Give yourself ample time when searching. If your current worker has walked off the job, you are still better off taking the necessary steps to hire right.

Skipping certain steps could lead to much worse problems than the time you will need to rehire. Give yourself at least two weeks to find someone. The time element depends on what you are in need of and what you are willing to pay. If you have unusual hours, or if you're offering a lower salary, the search could take extra time. Nothing works as fast as offering a great salary, but, of course, not everyone can afford to offer a higher salary. Nor does salary guarantee the right person.

I had one very prominent client who wanted to know what salary to offer for two different positions that he needed filled. I informed him of the going rates. He then asked what it would take to offer someone a salary which would be hard to walk away from. I made my suggestions, and he accepted them. That, of course, made it possible for him to interview those most qualified.

However, even with salary no problem, you must know what you are looking for. Let's review some of the steps and some of the techniques that will expedite the search and help assure a right choice in the end. The first organized step in hiring is to decide what you want. Analyze your need, which we have already discussed in the previous chapter.

Job descriptions

The next step is to prepare a realistic job description. Then use the appropriate job title, one that everyone in your area will understand at once. Don't advertise for a maid if you're looking for a housekeeper, nor a nanny if all you need is a part-time sitter.

Job titles open up a whole new can of worms in the nanny industry. The nanny industry is taking great strides and steps to help set uniform standards for training nannies. The term has been misused for as long as it has been used in this country.

For the first few years in business, I, too, often misused the term "nanny." In the beginning, I would advertise for a nanny. There are many who fought that and declared that a person should have to earn that title. Just as I had to complete four years of college and a specialized training program before I could be a certified teacher, a nanny is expected to have special training. At the agency, I soon eliminated reference to placing nannies, unless I did happen to have trained nannies on file. Periodically, I did.

That leads to another area of controversy: training. Many nanny schools have popped up during the past five years, and even more in the last three years. Some schools offer an extensive full-time, two-year training program. Others offer six to eight weeks of training, which sometimes consists of three-hour classes that meet once a week.

It's a known fact that there is an extreme shortage of trained nannies. When you look for child care, know that there are very few trained nannies available. If an agency professes to offer nannies, ask the definition of a nanny. If the agency cites training, inquire about the school. Some nanny placement agencies are giving a psychological test and declaring the applicant's competence in caring for children based on the results of that test. Consider your sources before hiring.

Job titles

By this time, you are probably wondering just how to title your job. Here are some samples that might work for you.

If you are a parent and are going to be at home and need additional help, you can classify the job Mother's

Helper. If you need child care while you are away, you can use the term "experienced sitter needed." Just because the nation is going crazy over trained nannies, does not mean that there are not good sitters out there with a great deal of experience.

A very simple form that should get you started in defining your job description is shown on pages 98 & 99.

It has already been established in this book that the first step in finding help is determining what needs to be done. The forms shown will help you organize that process.

Finding help

Once you know what you want, the next step is to let your needs be known and to attract applicants. The following sources will help you in locating help.

Yellow Page listings and child care services.
Look under these headings:
Child Care
Child Guidance
Information and Referral - Sitting Services

Nurses
Nurses – Practitioners
Nurses - Registries
Physicians
Physicians – Pediatric
Schools - Preschools and Kindergarten – Academic
Sitting Services

Newspaper Classified Advertising Listings.

Check listings for Child Care Services and Domestic Help under the following headings:
Child Care
Domestic Work Wanted
Help Wanted - Domestic

Yellow Page Listings for Senior Care Services.

Boarding Homes
Day Care Centers
Home Health Services
Nurses
Nurses - Practitioners
Nurses – Registries
Nursing Homes

How long does it take to find someone...

    Nursing Home Referral and
       Information Services
    Physicians
    Physicians – Geriatric
    Rest Homes
    Retirement and Life Care Communities
       and Homes
    Senior Citizen Services
    Sheltered Care Homes
    Sitting Services
    Social Service Organizations

    Of course, when you're in Arizona, get a copy of ***Options*** - *A Directory of Child and Senior Services* (Published by Five Star Publications)

Ad placement

    You can let your needs be known directly through ads in your local papers. After filling out the Job Description

form, you are ready to place your ad. Include these important items:
1. Provide a job title
2. Give a brief job description
3. Give general crossroads of job location
4. State a salary range
5. State days and hours required
6. State a non-smoker if required

Because advertising can be quite costly, keep your ads brief and to the point. Some papers will allow you to abbreviate certain words. If abbreviating is allowed, the ad taker will advise which words are most appropriate for abbreviating.

Also, when you place your ad, you will want to give your callers a complete job description. A job requiring someone to run errands will eliminate callers who do not drive. By phone, you can weed out as many unqualified callers as possible so that you can devote your time to interviewing only those most qualified applicants.

The sample ads on pages 31 & 32 provide the information needed about the position while keeping the advertising cost to a minimum.

How long does it take to find someone...

In the Phoenix area, I have found that it is best to advertise in the main Phoenix paper on Sunday and Wednesday in the Domestic Help Wanted column. This may vary in your area. You'll need to check with your local paper to learn which days and columns are best. Not all papers provide a Domestic Help category, so you may need to place your ad in the General Help Wanted section.

When I was searching for clients, I would advertise positions in the major Phoenix paper, but would advertise in the smaller city papers for positions in their specific areas. For example, if there was a position open in Scottsdale, I would advertise in the local Scottsdale paper to attract people wanting to work in their own vicinity. It has been my experience that applicants who accept a position too far from their residence soon tire of commuting. There is little chance of their changing residence, especially if they have children in school.

Ad samples

1. Mother's Helper needed. Work 3pm-6pm, Monday-Friday. $6.00/hr. near Stapley & Brown. Own car, non-smoker, & reference required.

Nannies, Maids & More

2. Housekeeper/Cook - Monday-Friday 12 noon - 8 pm. 35th St./Shea - up to $250/week. Exp. & ref. required.

3. Live-in sitter needed. Care for two infants. Tuesday-Saturday. $800/month plus benefits. Exp. & ref. required.

4. Cheerful and professional housekeeper/cook needed, live-in, cook/clean for mature couple, private quarters. $18,000-$25,000/yr. Exp. & Ref. a must.

5. Trained Nanny to live in and care for 2 yr. old. Monday-Friday. Must drive, have experience, references, and be non-smoker. Salary up to $1,000/month.

6. Exp. Houseman/Chauffeur. Cook, clean, and drive for professional couple. Private quarters. $30,000/yr. Exp. and ref. a must.

7. Experienced Laundress, MWF 9am-3pm. $7.50/hr. Paradise Valley area. Needed now! References required.

I think you get the general idea. Your phone

number or P.O. Box number would be included in each ad. If you require that applicants respond to a P.O. Box, you limit some of your response. If you want to use a phone number, you can always hire an answering service and they can assign a number for your use. This eliminates some of the risk of giving out your home or office number.

I have seen some ads that take up to 30 or more lines. I don't feel that is necessary. If you have the money, and want to list all details, then that's fine. But no matter how much you say in your ad, you are still going to have to pre-screen your calls.

Give yourself ample time to search. Not only may you not be happy with the first inquiries, you may find that your ideal candidate has changed his/her mind at the last minute.

Don't rely just on advertising

The following list will provide you with alternative sources for finding household help. Most of these are free, just time consuming. Remember that most people who come referred from these sources, do not come screened. A good rule of thumb is: Never leave screening to someone else's discretion.

1. **D.E.S.** The state Department of Economic Security may offer a free public employment service. It would probably list all types of jobs, such as opportunities in clerical, professional, and household employment. It is my understanding that no screening is done. Determine what similar service is available in your state.

2. **CHURCHES OR SYNAGOGUES.** Some places of worship offer an employment service. The Mormon church is the first one to come to mind. Some offer bul-

letin boards, or newsletters in which you can place an ad. Some ministers or rabbis might even make an announcement at a service. Others may shy away from this practice for fear they are acting more as an employment agency than anything else.

3. **COLLEGES, UNIVERSITIES, OR HIGH SCHOOLS.** Most schools either have a job placement service or an area where job listings can be posted. This is normally a free service provided to the community. This is an ideal place to search for part-time help.

4. **RADIO STATIONS.** Some radio stations will announce job opportunities over the air. There's a Spanish-speaking radio station in Arizona that lists job openings on a weekly basis. If you are going to use a station where a language other than English is spoken, you might ask the announcer to include in the description what language is required to be spoken and understood on the job.

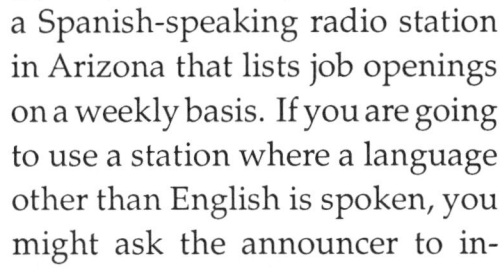

5. **TELEVISION.** Arizona viewers have the chance twice a week to find out about jobs in the community. The program is called *Where the Jobs Are.* Those jobs that are aired on TV are jobs listed with the Department of Economic Security, Job Placement Division. Check with your local D.E.S. office to see if a program of similar nature is offered in your area.

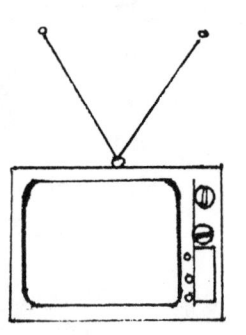

Time element

How long does it take to find household help? We still haven't answered that question completely. Sometimes families push agencies to the point of not giving them the proper time to screen applicants. If you approach an agency and even if you search on your own, take the time necessary to pre-screen. Give yourself ample screening time.

If your job has no unusual requirements (I found

that few do have), then there's a good chance of finding someone in one to two weeks. The more complicated the need, the more you get away from a full-time job, and in a job offering part time of less than twenty hours a week, the more difficult the search.

I found the search for live-in couples to take the longest of all requests. Finding two competent workers who happen to be married to each other and who have live-in experience was very difficult. A good two to three months is generally required for finding a live-in couple.

I learned a valuable lesson from one of my clients who had years of household hiring experience. She told me that it was difficult to get two good workers in a married couple. If was her observation that one would do most of the work, while the other just went along for the ride. So consider hiring two separate individuals. One may be a live-in and the other a live-out. You may find that you are getting more for your hiring dollar.

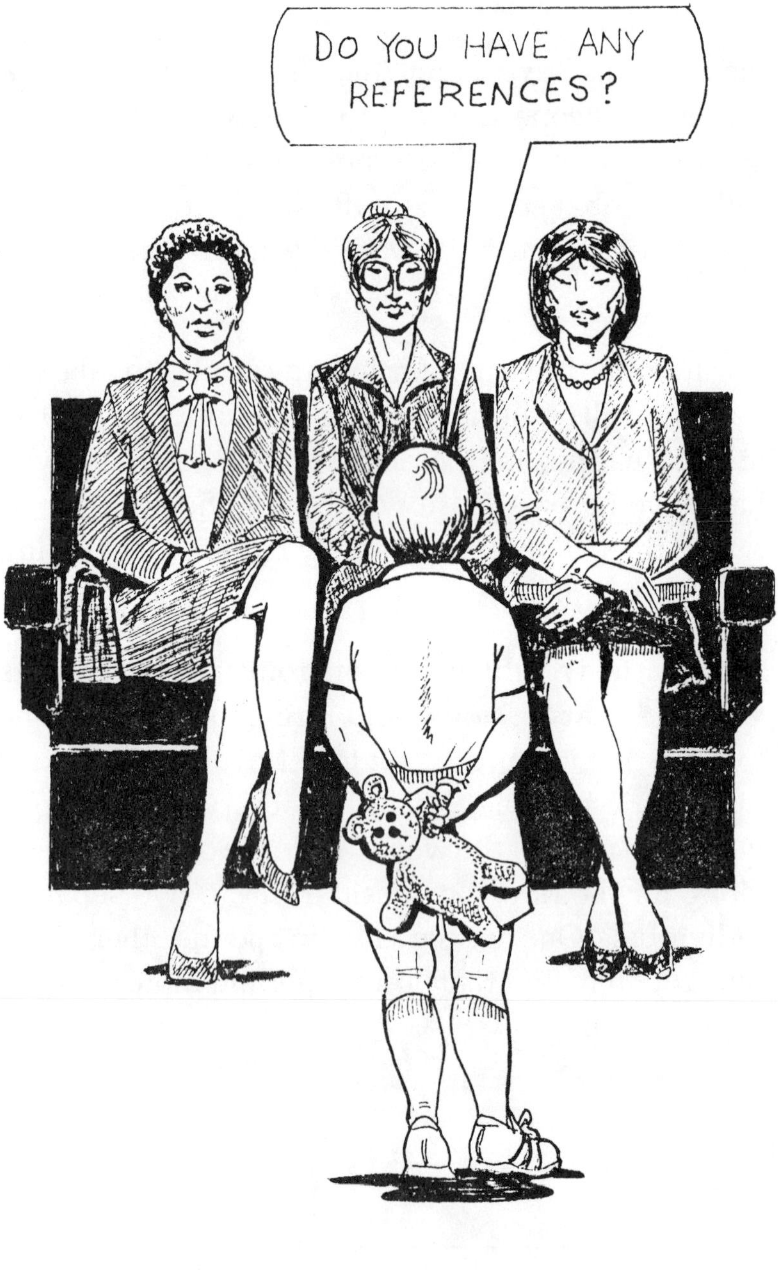
DO YOU HAVE ANY REFERENCES?

4

How can I know I've got the right person...

or - How do I manage the hiring process?

You have placed your ad and now comes the next big step, choosing the right applicant—not an easy task. Take your time and act thoughtfully as the replies come in.

Pre-screening calls

Before setting up any interviews, be sure to pre-screen your calls. Establish job qualifications and then ask each caller if he or she meets your requirements.

Qualifications will depend on your expectations and what the job requires. Generally speaking, look for these qualifications when hiring. Ask each caller if he or she meets these requirements:
- One year of work-related experience
- Excellent verifiable work references
- Reliable transportation
- A home phone
- Willingness to make at least a one-year job commitment (unless it is a temporary or short-term position)
- Living within a ten-mile radius of the job
- Physical exam within the last year, or a willingness to have one taken.

I had these qualifications posted in my agency office. Thus, if applicants felt they could bypass us on the phone, they were soon confronted with reality once they entered the office.

Let me say a little more about two of the above categories, the physical exam and having a home phone.

THE PHYSICAL EXAM. The AIDS scare has everyone concerned, especially those hiring care givers. A basic physical exam should cover any communicable diseases. True, physical exams can be costly. Most people looking for work are not in the position to pay for a physical exam. If you require a physical exam, you are probably going to have to be willing to pay for it. If you pay for it, you can have your personal physician give the exam. You can direct the doctor as to the areas you want checked and tested. Expect to pay no less than $100. AIDS tests are quite costly. What you require depends on how well screened you really want your care giver.

One of my clients spent $300 on a very complete physical exam for a sitter. The sitter was marvelous. My client couldn't sing enough praises. Shortly after, however, the sitter's husband was transferred to California. Be aware that your efforts at screening, which give you great peace of mind, do not guarantee that the person will stay forever, much less a year.

A HOME PHONE. In this day and age of playing phone tag, it's hard enough to get hold of a person with a phone, much less one without. Candidates inquiring about work, without a phone, often left us frustrated and out in the cold as we tried to line up interviews. Sometimes changes were necessary. Clients had changes come up, and periodically an applicant had a legitimate reason for not being able to interview. Message numbers often meant fruitless efforts to get in touch with the worker. If there was that much difficulty in just lining up the interview, imagine the problems if you hire someone without a phone. There will be times when you might need to make changes. That doesn't mean to say that all people without phones are not worth hiring. It just says that the likelihood for problems to pop up is much greater when you hire someone who does not have a phone.

Pre-screening by phone will save both you and the caller valuable time. Keep the list of requirements by your phone. Remember you're saving time eliminating unqualified candidates.

You may have noted that I did not list educational history as a job requirement. You may have strong feelings about an educational background. But remember that finding help is hard, and the more you require, the harder the search. Quality, well-educated caretakers are hard to come by. You will need to select the most qualified from what is available.

Interviewing

I have had clients who interviewed in their office, my agency's office, or in their own home. You must decide what is best for you. Remember that applicants calling directly have not yet been screened. As a safety precaution, you may choose to use your office. If you do not have a suitable office space, you may want to set up the interviews at a local restaurant or hotel conference room. If you have used your home phone number in your ad, then applicants do have the number from the ad, but not necessarily your address. You may not want them to know where you live in case your final decision does not result in hiring them.

Try setting up three or four appointments per day, giving yourself forty-five to sixty minutes per interview. If you are using forms like the application for employment on pages 100 & 101, remember that it will take the applicant at least fifteen to thirty minutes to fill out the forms.

When you are setting up the interviews, ask each candidate to come prepared with names, addresses, and phone numbers of three past employers and two non-related references. It helps save you time and also allows you to evaluate how adequately they follow your initial instructions.

APPLICATION FOR EMPLOYMENT: The application for employment should be fully completed by the applicant. Leaving blanks generally leads to a long or frustrating search for the information when it is most needed.

See the sample application pages 100 & 101.

Former address and Social Security number are important for credit checks, which are more difficult without this information. Make it easy on yourself the first time around. Take the time to review the application before the applicants leave. If they do not have all the information, it can always be phoned in to you.

Make sure also that the application is signed. Without a signature, you may be unable to verify the information. When checking references with large companies, you may find that most, if not all, require a copy of the employee's signature authorizing the release of the information requested.

When you interview an applicant, don't try to change what is there. This can be compared to selecting a marriage partner. I once had a girl come into my office who truly had wonderful references. I did notice that she seemed to have a body odor, along with unruly styled, somewhat greasy hair. But she was so nice. Her references spoke highly of her, and I genuinely liked her. I really wanted to try to help her. (What I really thought was that I could turn her into a Cinderella.) I strongly encouraged a fresh haircut and told her that the client strongly emphasized how important proper hygiene was to her. I thought this would be a kind way of saying, "Take a bath and get your hair cut and styled..." I lined up the interview. She promised she would get a haircut. I had her show up at my office before the interview. She was so excited, she told me she would stop at the beauty salon on the way to my office. If she did, not much resulted from it. I just couldn't send her out. So I had to cancel the interview. This was one case I discussed with my husband. He pointed out that even if she had had her hair styled, personal hygiene and grooming habits do not change overnight, and that soon the old habits would reappear. Don't think that personal habits change easily. Values and personal habits run deep and are not easily changed or modified.

INTERVIEW IMPRESSION SHEET: (See page 102). The importance of each area covered on the application will vary by employer depending on your requirements and expectations. This sheet is helpful to those who are unsure of what to ask during an interview. (See completed sample on page 103). It also ensures that you give each candidate a fair shake at the job by asking the same questions of each.

No matter how many people I interviewed, I always utilized the interview impression sheet. I found it most helpful when reviewing the applications. I always filled out this form as I interviewed. Some of my counselors felt more comfortable completing it after the interview. I found, however, that when one waits, there are so many distractions that come along, and one forgets important data. Of course, you might be interviewing only a few candidates, whereas we interviewed on an ongoing basis. You, on the other hand, are most likely interviewing for one specific job.

Following are the main points on the sheet and a few comments on each.

1. **Appropriate appearance.** A neat appearance is necessary, regardless of the job.

2. **Prior work experience.** At least one year is generally preferred, but it is not mandatory. I received dozens, if not hundreds, of calls from

women applying for housekeeping positions believing their personal home cleaning experience qualified them. I had poor results placing women who lacked professional experience, although it should not necessarily eliminate them. If you have time to train them properly, it can work out most satisfactorily. You may phrase your initial question by asking if they have been employed as a housekeeper. If you just ask if they have had housekeeping experience, nine out of ten will say yes. The majority are referring to the cleaning of their own home.

3. **Prior job stability.** Stability and job longevity are two of the most important factors to consider in your search. Watch carefully for job hoppers – those holding four to six jobs in the past year.

4. **Enthusiasm/motivation.** Some employers are in search of self-starters, while others are happy with good workers who need regular supervision and direction. You must decide what is most important to you. You are the judge of the enthusiasm applicants display during the interview, and you must question their motivation. Atti-

tudes come in here as well. To me, a worker who lacks a good attitude, but has many good references, lacks the key ingredient for a good employee.

5. **Maturity/poise.** You have to judge how well the applicants present themselves during the interview.

6. **Career goals.** Ask what their career goals are and how long, as well as why, they plan to do this kind of work.

7. **Appropriate ability.** Again, you must use your own sound judgment. Do you believe this person is capable of doing the job?

8. **Overall strengths.** (See item 9.)

9. **Overall weaknesses.** Most applicants are intrigued by these two questions. Many have never been asked about and will have to give some thought as to their strengths or weaknesses. One answer stands out in my mind with an applicant who was applying for a houseman's job. When

asked about his overall weaknesses, he quickly responded with "Chocolate." (Mine, too!)

See completed Interview Impression Work Sheet page 103.

Checking references

Many people question the validity of checking references, assuming that applicants will not provide names of anyone who might give an unfavorable review. However, having screened over a thousand applicants yearly, I have found that the reference forms I designed prove quite useful in evaluating a potential worker. The forms have elicited some very critical evaluations from both employers and "friends." When asked to write a letter of recommendation, many responded with only favorable comments, but by answering specific questions, they had a basis for evaluation. Expect many of the larger corporations to respond with only verification of employment and salary. Following are samples of forms mailed through my agency and responses received.

See sample reference forms completed on pages 105 & 107.

Verification of employment and salary is another indicator that the candidate is supplying you with truthful information, though it may turn up some surprises, too. I had one young candidate who was anxious to work. I noticed on her application that she shared transportation with her mother. When I questioned her reliability, I wanted reassurance that the sharing of one vehicle would not interfere with her being to work on time each day. She assured me there would be no problem. I still had my doubts. When I brought up the possibility of her mother needing the car, she reluctantly told me that she has access to her mother's chauffeur. It would be the chauffeur who would drive her to and from work. After the initial shock wore off (it took a lot to surprise me, for over the years there was much that did not come as a surprise... this did), I told her that it might not work out, because the job required being able to run errands. She emphasized that the chauffeur would help her with her errand running. Amazing...could this really be? After her departure, my secretary informed me that, indeed, there was a huge limousine parked in front of my office.

She begged for a chance at a job. She stated on her application that she had graduated from high school. Through high school verification, I learned that she hadn't graduated from high school. If memory serves me, I believe she hardly ever showed at school and didn't make it past her freshman year. Thus her sincere efforts were lost through her inability to give accurate information. Check all courses of information given to you.

Also, have each candidate complete five reference forms. (Three employer and two non-related character reference forms.) When all forms have been completed, check to be sure both the application and the reference forms have been signed by the applicant. In order to do a verification of the information supplied, you must have the applicant's permission. For a credit check, a Social Security number must be given. Verification is easier if you get a former address and Zip Code, if possible.

How can I know I've got the right person...

See sample Employer Reference sheet on page 104. See sample Character Reference sheet on page 105.

Last, but not least, comes the question: How can I find someone who will not harm our children or steal us blind? No one person, agency, or book can guarantee that neither of the above will happen, but the following three steps will give you some peace of mind.

CREDIT CHECK: Besides contacting references, you can do a credit check. My agency was a member of a credit reporting agency. I paid monthly dues and was able to call in and get oral verification. If you are not a member of a credit reporting agency, you may be able to pay a non-member fee and get a report. One agency that I know of charges an $8 fee to non-members.

BONDING: Another major concern is bonding. Many people are unaware that bonding covers only proven theft but does not cover any act of violence. The accused party must be taken to a court of law and must be proven guilty of the crime before you can collect on a bond. When the court rules the person guilty, you should be able to collect from the bonding company up to the value of the property stolen, provided it does not exceed the amount of the bond. For example, if a $10,000 ring is stolen, but the person was bonded for only $5,000, then $5,000 would be all that you could recover.

Check your local insurance company for bond rates. If you are unsure of whom to call, contact your homeowners or car insurance agent who should be able to refer you to an appropriate agency.

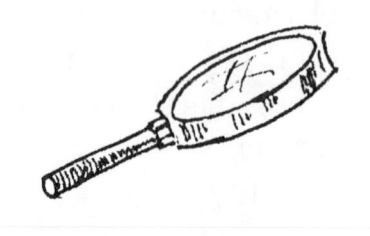

FBI INVESTIGATION: This topic brings out the frustration in most people hiring household help. Most individual employers are unable to obtain an FBI report about a potential employee. There are agencies that, for a fee, will do the investigation for you. Unless the employer is licensed to obtain an FBI report on the individual to be hired, then candidates must request their own report. The current cost given by the FBI is $14 for an individual to obtain his or her own report. The individuals must be able to prove with sufficient ID that they are who they say they are. They will need to send in a set of their fingerprints with their request. They can have themselves fingerprinted through the local sheriff's office. The sheriff or police office will direct them to the closest facility for fingerprinting. The FBI report takes up to six weeks. Most people have immediate needs for hiring. FBI reports are time consuming, but that option is there.

If you would like a candidate whom you are going to hire to obtain an FBI report, the following will be needed:

1. Written letter by the individual requesting his or her own report.

2. Satisfactory proof of personal ID, consisting of full name, date and place of birth.

3 Set of rolled inked fingerprint impressions, placed upon an official fingerprint card or form. This card or form is available through most law enforcement agencies.

4. Fee. At this time, it is $14, which must be in the form of a certified check or money order, payable to the Treasurer of the United States. Personal checks are not accepted.

5. Address to which the report is to be mailed.

Address the request letter to:
FBI, Identification Division
Washington, DC 20537-9700

Expect this report to take a minimum of six weeks.

DRIVING RECORD: Checking on driving record. You should know what kind of driving history the applicant has, especially if driving is expected on the job. Even if it is not, you never know when an emergency will arise and require a family member to be driven somewhere.

How to obtain a driving history. Either you or

the individual you are about to hire can request a copy of the person's driving record. The following procedures are followed in Arizona, but I believe the procedures should be the same in most states, though the fees may vary.

Driving records obtained from the individual:

1. Each individual can request a copy of his or her driving history from the Motor Vehicle Department. (When searching for the phone number, look under Department of Transportation in the phone book.)

2. The individual needs to supply the following information:
    a. Individual's full name
    b. Birth date
    c. Driver's license number

The fee to be sent with the request in Arizona is: $2 for information covering the past thirty-nine months and $5 for the record covering the past five years. There is a $5 charge to have a clearance letter written. If the request is made in person, the fee is $3 for the thirty-nine-month record and $5 for the five-year report.

Driving records requests by employers by mail:

1. Write to the Motor Vehicle Department and request the driving record of the person you would like to hire.

2. Include the following information:
    a. Individual's full name
    b. Birth date
    c. Driver's license number
    d. Your notarized signature
    e. Your reason for this request

Turn-around time for getting this information is four to six weeks. If you contact the Motor Vehicle Department, they might have a request form they can mail you. Ask for several!

(No one said this was going to be easy!)

CHAUFFEUR'S LICENSE: If your hired help are expected to run any errands for you in their own private cars, they will need to have or obtain a Chauffeur's License. Failure to have the license for any paid employee who chauffeurs your children (or anyone at your request), or who runs errands for you in the employee's car could result in the insurance provider not covering any incident which resulted while they were acting as an unlicensed chauffeur.

This whole area of liability and insurance coverage should be checked very carefully with your insurance agent (or attorney, if you have one). For example, one adviser told me that the employer should have his or her name added on the employee's automobile insurance policy if the employee would be driving at the request of the employer. Again, *be sure of the requirements of insurance and the conditions covered.*

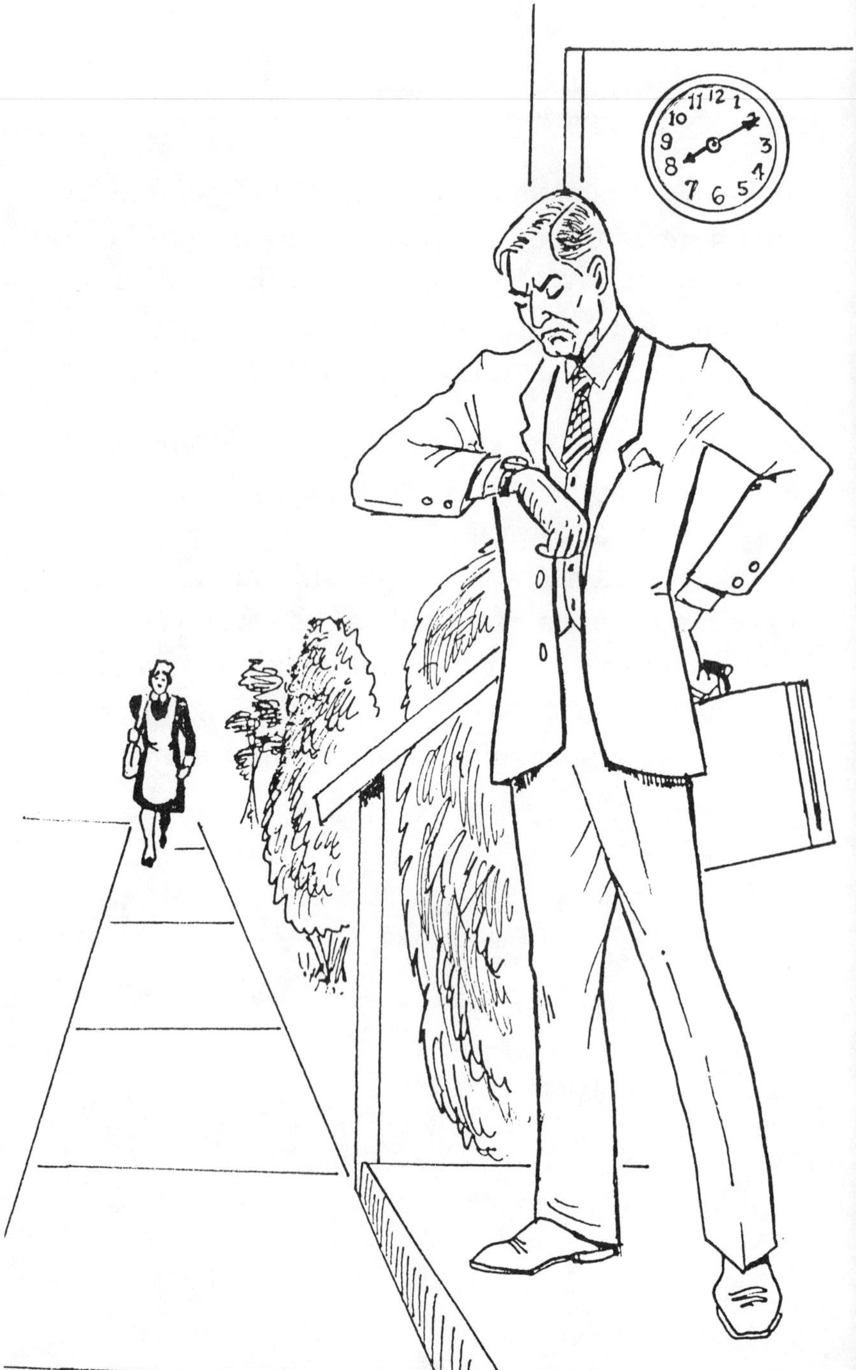

5

I've got someone, but I want to let her (or him) go...

Think twice before you fire...in fact, go back to square one and think about what is involved in terminating employment.

If the termination—either on your part or the employee's—arises from changed circumstances, there is no problem. The agreed-upon notice is given and references are promised.

In the case of unsatisfactory work, the situation is different. If causes of termination were spelled out in the work contract, generally they must be observed. Prior warning must be given and documented. The date of termination can be set in regard to the offense. Frequent tardiness might well result only in eventual termination, whereas dishonesty would merit immediate dismissal.

If your state department has a handbook of employment regulations, obtain a copy and follow its regulations. In any event, stop and consider the following before letting someone go.

A common cause for firing is simple: The gusto is gone. The employee started out so well, but the work quality is now lacking. That is why I stress in the initial interview: Let your potential employees know what you expect from them. Let them know what disappointed you about past household help. If the gusto is lacking, and if the force that was once

I've got someone, but I want to let her (or him) go...

there seems to be lost, first talk about it. Give the employees a second chance. If such chances have already been given, then you may be better off letting them go.

Letting an employee go

Why is it so hard to let help go? I have dealt with corporate leaders, who on a daily basis have to hire and fire in their offices, yet the thought of firing household help left them defenseless. Why?

Their greatest concerns were:

1. They might be left without help.

2. This person works for them personally, and there is a tendency for household workers to take on the role of a family member. The employer feels more as though he is firing Mom, rather than the nanny or the maid.

If you come to this situation, the cold, hard truth is: You need to decide whether it is going to be more productive for you to rehire or to accept unacceptable behaviors or conditions. This is where intelligent, thought-out interviewing helps you. During your initial interview you can let applicants know the kind of things that will cause the job to terminate. If you have communicated on different occasions that they need to work on those areas, and they haven't improved, then you have ample reason to dismiss them.

There should be a company that does nothing but fire people. A job not liked, but it must be done.

In agency work, I generally did not hear from a client or worker if the placement was successful. Times that led me to hearing from either of them generally resulted from unkept promises. Before you promise something, be prepared to live up to it or you jeopardize losing your help.

Preventive hiring and firing and quitting tips

Some household employees quit and others are asked to leave. Often, knowing the reasons that these two situations occur may help you avoid some problems. Here are some of the common reasons for firing an employee and tips on how you can foresee these problems by careful interviewing and thorough reference checking, as described in the preceding chapters.

Reasons for firing (or reasons for not hiring)

1. **Chronic lateness.**
   Applicant is late or changes appointment at the last minute

2. **Low quantity or poor quality of work performance.**
   Check the references for these most important details.

3. **Poor attitude.**
   Question candidates about why they want this job. Make sure the salary offered will meet their needs. Again, check the references for this problem.

4. **Personal/family problems.**
   Be attentive to any information on this subject divulged by the prospective employee or by the ref-

erences. Personal/family problems generally mean that the work will suffer either through worry, numerous phone calls, or absences.

In the interviewing process you can make it clear what you will expect of the applicant. Employees don't always have this same privilege and sometimes find themselves in a position they didn't bargain for. Following are some other common reasons why employees quit their jobs.

Reasons for quitting (or what a smart employer doesn't do)

1. The employer does not allow the employee to work the hours originally agreed upon.

2. The job description changes and the employee is then required to do more work than was expected from the initial job description.

3. The employee feels that he or she is not being treated with respect.

I've got someone, but I want to let her (or him) go...

4. The employer is having personal/family problems and is creating a difficult work atmosphere for the employee.

5. The employee is not given positive feedback about job performance.

6. The employee did not receive a raise within the agreed-upon time.

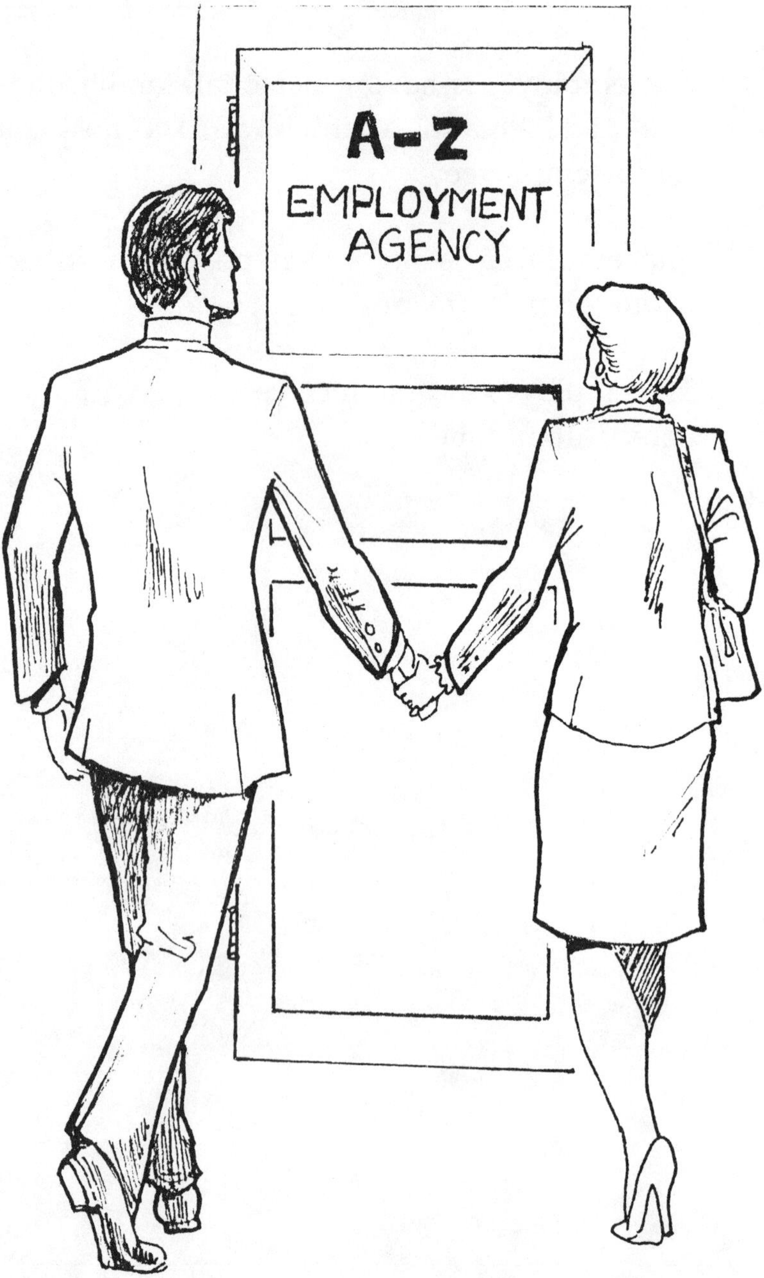
A-Z
EMPLOYMENT AGENCY

6

I want to use an agency...

You can use placement agencies to locate household employees for the same reasons that businesses turn to commercial agencies. An agency brings experience and expertise to the search. It commands a wider field of candidates. It screens and tests potential employees. It guards the employer's privacy. And above all, it relieves the employer of much of a difficult and time-consuming task. Using an agency trades expertise and time for money.

Agencies exist on the fees they charge for their services. In effect, the employer and the agency are entering into a business agreement. The agency has a right to expect that the employer is seriously looking for help—not just dabbling around to see what's out there. And the client has a right to know the qualifications of the service he or she is buying.

Selecting an agency

Buyer beware. Learn about the agency you will be using. Here are steps you should take.

☑ 1. **Read the agreement or contract carefully.** Who will be paying the fees?

☑ 2. **Ask to see some references from past or current clients.**

☑ 3. **Check to see how the agency is licensed.** Ask if it is licensed through the Industrial Commission in your area. Arizona employ-

I want to use an agency...

ment agencies are regulated by the Industrial Commission, but make note that not all agencies must be licensed through this agency. If an agency charges a placement fee to the worker, then the agency is required by Arizona law to be licensed through the Commission. If an agency is not charging any part of a placement fee to the worker, then the license is not necessary. If an agency is licensed, it does not necessarily mean that it is charging an applicant a fee. I had my agency licensed in order to promote professionalism within my industry. Licensing also gives both the applicant and the client a certain peace of mind in knowing that they are dealing with a licensed agency. The license actually best protects the worker placed. If an agency misrepresents any part of a placement·fee, it jeopardizes its state license. A test governing hiring laws must be passed in order to obtain a license.

☑ 4. **Ask if the agency is bonded.** Arizona requires a licensed employment agency to maintain a $5,000 bond. The bond is there to protect those paying a fee. This bond is another form of insurance for the client paying a fee. The bond also helps ensure that the agency honors guarantees connected with the fees charged. If the agency is not licensed through the state industrial commission, then it is not obligated to have a bond. It's still a good practice for an agency to follow. It is to your benefit to be dealing with a licensed and bonded agency when you enter into a written contract.

☑ 5. **Check with the Better Business Bureau to see whether any unsatisfied claims have been filed with the Bureau.**

☑ 6. **Make sure that guarantees are spelled out.** Know what happens in the event a placement does not succeed. I spent hundreds, if not thousands, of dollars in having professional contracts designed by attorneys. One of my clients, who happened to be an attorney, wanted to review my contract before entering into business with me—a smart practice on his part. He had contacted another service and was leery of all the loopholes in their contract. I felt my contract had covered

I want to use an agency...

all areas of concerns felt by both client and agency. After reviewing my documents, the attorney agreed that the contract was a well-written agreement that let both parties know exactly where they stood during the life of the agreement.

☑ 7. **Damage.** Determine what happens if the person placed does any type of harm or damage. Most agencies will not hold any liability for this, but make sure that that is covered in the agreement. You may want to check with your homeowners insurance agent to see what he or she can offer you. Insurance is not cheap.

☑ 8. **Screening.** Ask what type of screening the agency does. Do you have access to the references checked? How are references checked? Is it by phone or mail? Is it written or oral? Ask to see copies of all references. Many of our clients never asked to see references. Do ask, there is nothing wrong in calling some of the references yourself. You are most likely not under any obligation, (you shouldn't be) when hiring through an agency. Make sure before hiring that the applicant checks out with you. Remember, you are making the final decision to hire, not the agency.

☑ 9. **Payroll.** Determine whose payroll this worker will be on. Many agencies act strictly as independent contractors when they place temporary or permanent help. Otherwise the agency is hired for the purpose of finding, locating, and screening potential household workers. They do not hire or act in any manner in behalf of the client. Many workers do not want to be on a payroll. They want to work as independent contractors. I can't discourage this practice enough. There are certain responsibilities by law that you, the employer, can't avoid. Doing so can cause future financial disasters.

☑ 10. **Employee contracts.** Find out if the agency has contract forms to use with employees. If not, you may want to design one yourself or seek an attorney to assist you in drawing up an employee contract. An employee contract

I want to use an agency...

leaves nothing to chance. It spells out the job description, paid holidays, benefits, reviews, raises, and causes for termination.

Sample termination causes might include the following: Being tardy to work three times, not calling in to report an absence, or whatever else you might feel to be cause for dismissal.

One important clause to include is a provision for quitting. For example, both parties agree to give a two-week notice of termination. If a person could be fired, you'll need to word the contract accordingly. Just as a contract protects you from someone just walking off the job, it also gives the employees peace of mind that you are not going to drop them like a hot potato if "Grandma" moves in and they are no longer needed to fill the job.

☑ 11. **Assure yourself that the agency will protect your identity until you are ready to interview.**

Remember that most towns, no matter how large, are basically a small world for hiring household help. I had one client who was in need of a governess. The day after I advertized the position for an experienced governess, I had three people in my office waiting to be interviewed. The first had worked for my client three years earlier, the second had worked for him briefly and was dismissed, and the third was still employed by him. All client information being confidential, his name was never given out to the applicants. They only knew that they were applying for a governess job. It was through their applications that I discovered they had worked for him. Another reason for being good to your employees. If you aren't, word travels fast in the world of household help.

☑ 12. **Resumes.** Can the agency provide resume forms? Very few workers in the domestic or child care field are trained in writing resumes. You may want to give an applicant a blank resume form to fill out. In the field of hiring professional staff for corporations, you would turn away those without resumes. Once again, though, you need to work with what is out there. This is not a put-down on

I want to use an agency…

household workers. The standards are coming. Professional standards come with professional treatment and better pay. If you expect to hire only those qualified for the job, then better pay and benefits will have to follow.

☑ 13. **Determine what fees are charged to find workers.**

Are there any deposits or up-front charges? If there are, what happens if a placement does not occur? Are these deposits refundable? If the deposit is non-refundable, can it be applied at another time?

When is the fee due?

Is the fee split with the worker?

☑ 14. **Inquire about guarantees.** Does the agency offer a guarantee if for some reason the employee does not work out? If so, for how long is the guarantee effective? How many replacements will be made during the guaranteed time?

☑ 15. **Ask where interviews will take place.** Will you interview in your home, in the agency office, or in a designated interviewing place? Some of our clients preferred to have the initial interview at their office or ours. Some met at restaurants.

☑ 16. **Ask about bonding.** Is the agency bonded? Are the applicants bonded? If not, how do you get them bonded? Is bonding necessary?

Most people who employ someone in their home are concerned about bonding and this concern may extend to the agency as well as the worker. All state-licensed agencies must carry a bond. In Arizona, the amount is $5,000. However this bond covers only the agency; and many agencies do not have their workers bonded.

(For bonding of household employees, see Chapter 4.)

☑ 17. **Ask how much screening the agency does.** At one time I thought that most agencies did a good job of screening. That soon was shown to be a myth. The number one complaint coming from clients that used other services was screening and lack of it. They never seemed satisfied with the screening

I want to use an agency...

done. If you are hiring several replacements a year, then it's time to evaluate where the problem lies. Is it with the agency, the screening, or the conditions that prevail in the work environment?

☑ 18. **Will you, the employer, be screened?** Screening the employer is not an easy thing to do. But more and more agencies are screening the families in need of care as well as the care providers. One possible source of screening would be contacting the last hired worker and getting a reference for his or her employer. Nothing like switching roles.

(Are you still with me? Do you still want to hire household help? Is the thought becoming less appealing, each page you read?)

What to do about a service problem

If you have a problem with an employment service, FIRST try to work it out with the service. If this brings no satisfaction, the next step is to consult the licensing source. (One of the benefits of using a state licensed agency.) If the agency is not licensed, you can then seek the advice of an attorney.

Agency expectations

Agencies have expectations of the clients. Often it became a revelation in points of view as the agency and the client came together. Clients sometimes had little idea of their own role in the partnership of employer and agency.

For instance, many clients would come to me and not really know just what household help they needed. We would talk about their schedule, what they wanted done, and what they were willing to pay. Then we would discuss if what they wanted done was compatible with what they were paying, or were willing to pay.

Be aware that the more you expect from someone, the more you should be willing to pay. Keep in mind that if you want someone to do cooking, cleaning, and child care, you are expecting three jobs to be done by one person.

I want to use an agency…

During this day of specialization, I sometimes forget just how specialized we have become. One experience brought me up short. A client called and said she wanted someone to care for the children, pick them up from school, do laundry, keep the house tidy, do the ironing, and have a hot meal on the table for the children and husband and wife when they got home. When I informed her that she was expecting too much for what she wanted to pay, she responded with, "What do you mean, I'm expecting too much?… It's what the average wife has to do on a daily basis!"

Maybe, but perhaps that's one reason why marriages just don't make it…which leads me to another story. I always asked my clients how they had heard about my agency. When one client responded that she heard of me from her psychiatrists, I had to hold back my laughter. She then went on to explain that her husband was a doctor and he strongly felt that when he returned home from a long day at the office, he wanted all four youngsters in a presentable format, a hot meal on the table, and, of course, pleasant conversation. With four children of varying ages, the wife found the mission impossible. Most of her time was spent chauffeuring the children to their various lessons and little leagues. There was little time for a clean home, hot meals, and clean and sparkling children.

Her analyst recommended my service to help save her marriage. If she wanted to meet her husband's expectations, she needed a mother's helper—a mother's helper to give her relief, assistance, and make some sanity out of her life. We found her the mother's helper. I never claimed large miracles, just small ones.

My most unforgettable case (client)

Another example from my days as an agency head is probably the most outstanding in my mind. *Reader's Digest* always comes up with a story about someone's most unforgettable character. Well, this has to be one of my unforgettable clients (one of many).

This client called and needed child care for her, I believe it was three children, or was it two…anyway, children. She said her father was dying and that he lived in another state. She wanted desperately to be at his side. She needed a sitter immediately.

When it came to my agency fee, she agreed to charge part of the deposit on their charge card. So with the deposit paid, I was ready to go. I worked all day and into that night until I found her a quality sitter, ready to begin the next morning.

The next day in my office I was busy as usual when the day was just about over and my mind was on going home…when the sitter called to inform me that the client had left a note for her and for the client's husband. The note to the sitter said she was leaving her husband. The husband had called home around four o'clock and was surprised to hear a strange woman's voice. His first question was "Who are you?" After introductions were made by the sitter, he informed her that he was calling to take his wife out to dinner. The sitter felt there was something he needed knowing, and it was something that couldn't wait…She told him there was a note addressed to him…so he had her read it. Of course, notes like these cannot come as a total surprise, but a surprise it was, nonetheless.

The husband contacted me. I first told him the good news…I had found him the sitter. The bad news was that his wife charged the fee on his charge card.

I worked with him until other arrangements could be made...I just couldn't see hitting him up with a wife walking out on him and a placement fee all in the same day.

This story does have a happy ending. I found out several months later that the wife came back. She apparently needed time away. The thing that I found most disappointing was that she told me she was going to visit a dying parent...only to be told by her husband that the parent she spoke of had died several months before. I guess desperation can lead women (and men) to tell lies.

How does one screen for that?

Can you see the ad for trying to fill that job:

Wife with three kids wants to leave her husband immediately. Cook, clean, and care for kids, have hot meal on table for husband. Salary comparable to that of being a wife.

If husbands had to find someone to be a wife in the generic sense, they would soon find the replacement not easy, the cost unobtainable.

I want to use an agency...

Job Description Form

(See sample form on pages 98 & 99.)

The more specific you can be in your job description and in the interview, the better chance you have of filling the job with someone who has a chance of best meeting your expectations.

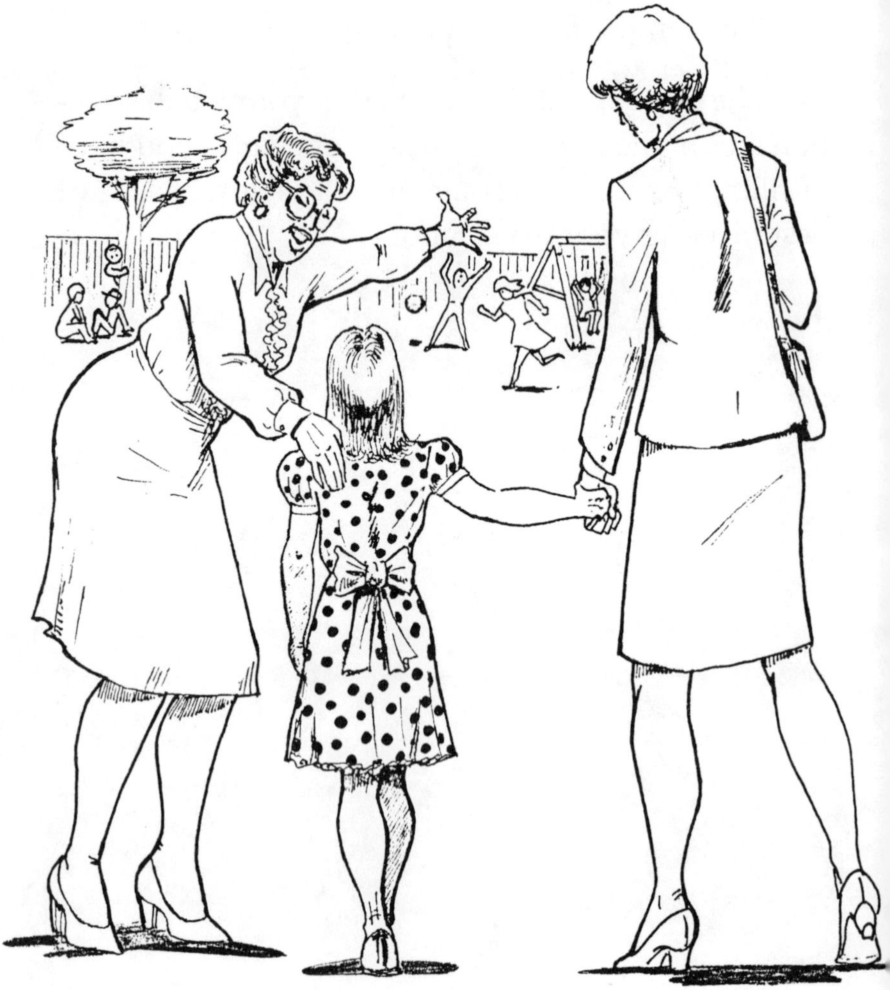

7

I want to use outside care...

The alternative to finding a care giver in the home is to use an outside care center. The range of such services is growing, particularly for older adults.

Selecting a care center

Whether you decide to choose a day care center (child or adult), family home day care, or a preschool, it is a good idea to visit several care providers or care centers, observe the environment and care provider's behavior, and conduct an interview before deciding on placement of your child or senior. Here are some questions you may want to ask of the care provider:

- What hours is care available?
- Is care available on holidays?
- What is the ratio of care providers to children or seniors?
- How do you screen your care providers?
- What qualification or education do you require of your care providers?
- Is the day well structured?
- What type of activities are planned?
- What is your philosophy regarding discipline?

I want to use outside care...

- What kind of lunch and/or snacks are served?

- Are there any restrictions on who is accepted for care (e.g., age, mental or physical handicaps, etc.)?

- Do you have a contract? If yes, ask for a copy.

- Are you licensed? The requirements may be different in different states. Look into the requirements and be sure they are met. In Arizona, for example, anyone who cares for more than four children other than their own must be licensed by the Arizona Department of Health Services.

- What kind of insurance do you carry to cover possible accidents or injuries to children/seniors under your care?

- What precautions are taken to ensure safety to those being cared for?

- Do you have an enclosed, safe area for outdoor activities?

- Do you have a swimming pool? If so, does it have a gate that is kept locked?

- What do you charge for day care?

- When is payment due?

- Do you expect payment for days child or senior is not brought to day care (i.e., holidays, vacations, sick days)?

Review the agency contract before signing it.

Ask who is responsible for insurance if someone gets hurt.

If you are having an agency or agencies help you in screening family home day care, find out what their screening process is; ask to see their forms; and find out how often they monitor the homes.

Other alternatives in child care

If the thought of a private sitter appeals to you,

I want to use outside care...

but you just can't afford it, consider the following:

Latch-key programs are offered in some school districts. Check with your local school to find out what after-school programs are offered. Also contact your local YMCA or YWCA. Many of the Y's offer after-school programs.

If your area has an information and referral service, contact them.

Many families consider home day cares. Arizona has more than 1,000 home day cares certified by the Department of Economic Security. State-licensed family home day cares are screened and licensed by the Department.

You may be eligible for family home day care at a reduced rate through your state's Department of Economic Security. Call the Department to check the financial guidelines for this eligibility. Such departments may offer a list that they utilize in screening potential family home day care providers. It would be useful in helping you choose a care provider.

If you do not qualify for the state aid, contact a service in your area that screens and places children in home day cares. The cost will be divided by the caretaker's ability to care for a certain number of children outside her own. Contact your local Department of Health Services to find out about laws governing child care givers in your area.

I have just learned, for example, that as of July 1, 1989, the Arizona Department of Health Services will be licensing large group family homes, which can care for five to ten children in a private home. There must be at least two adult caretakers where homes have six or more children. Options in child care continue to increase as the demand outstrips the traditional supply.

When you are looking for child care possibilities, referrals from friends are always best. However, if you don't have a referral to rely on, check with your local Department of Economic Security office or Department of Health Services.

I want to use outside care...

Child and senior care needs will only continue to soar, as both parents work or the home is being run by a single parent. Thus it is well to be aware of the alternatives so that you can choose the one best suited to your needs and resources.

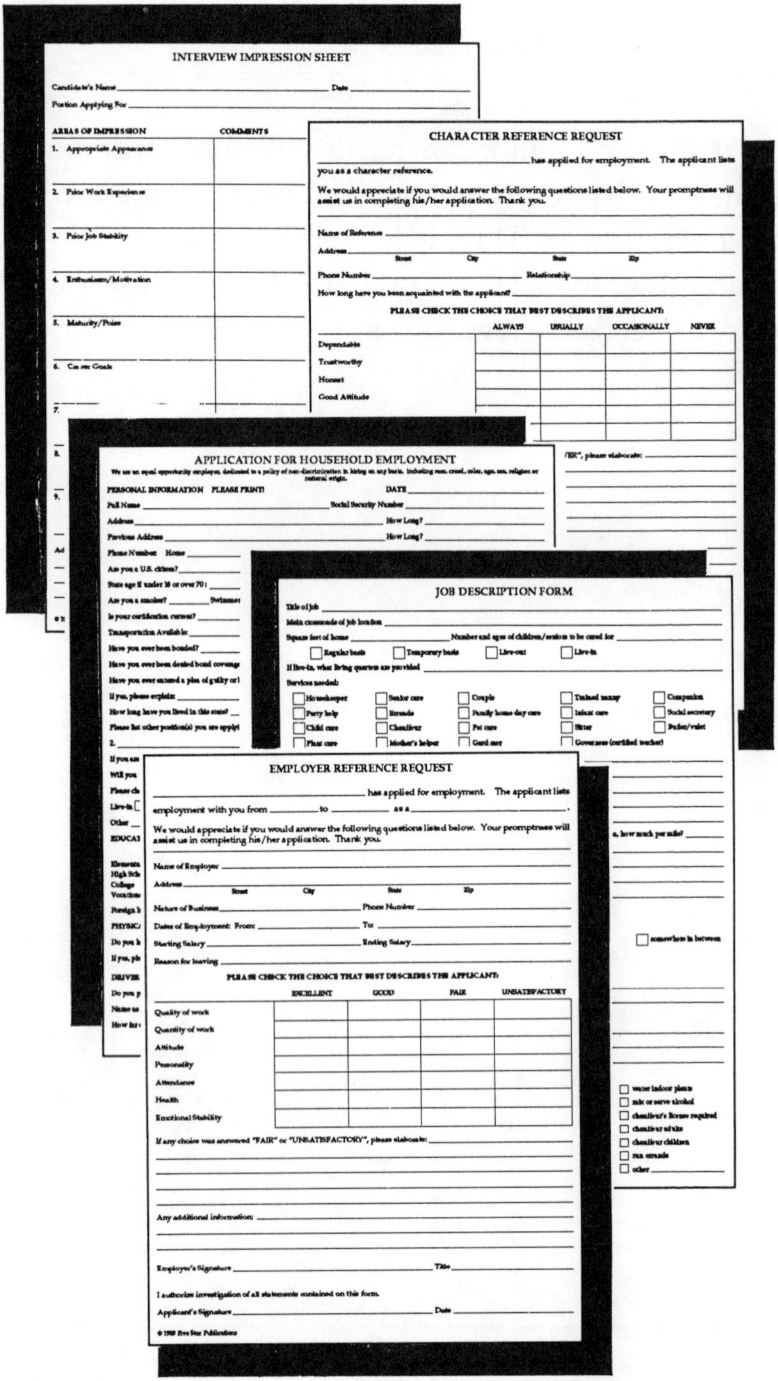

INTERVIEW IMPRESSION SHEET

Candidate's Name ____ Date ____

Position Applying For ____

AREAS OF IMPRESSION | COMMENTS

1. Appropriate Appearance

2. Prior Work Experience

3. Prior Job Stability

4. Enthusiasm/Motivation

5. Maturity/Poise

6. Career Goals

7.

8.

9.

CHARACTER REFERENCE REQUEST

____ has applied for employment. The applicant lists you as a character reference.

We would appreciate if you would answer the following questions listed below. Your promptness will assist us in completing his/her application. Thank you.

Name of Reference ____

Address ____ Street City State Zip

Phone Number ____ Relationship ____

How long have you been acquainted with the applicant? ____

PLEASE CHECK THE CHOICE THAT BEST DESCRIBES THE APPLICANT:

	ALWAYS	USUALLY	OCCASIONALLY	NEVER
Dependable				
Trustworthy				
Honest				
Good Attitude				

APPLICATION FOR HOUSEHOLD EMPLOYMENT

We are an equal opportunity employer, dedicated to a policy of non-discrimination in hiring on any basis, including race, creed, color, age, sex, religion or national origin.

PERSONAL INFORMATION PLEASE PRINT! DATE ____

Full Name ____ Social Security Number ____

Address ____ How Long? ____

Previous Address ____ How Long? ____

Phone Number: Home ____

Are you a U.S. citizen? ____

State age if under 18 or over 70: ____

Are you a smoker? ____

Is your certification current? ____

Transportation Available: ____

Have you ever been bonded? ____

Have you ever been denied bond coverage ____

Have you ever entered a plea of guilty or ____

If yes, please explain: ____

How long have you lived in this state? ____

Please list other position(s) you are applying

JOB DESCRIPTION FORM

Title of Job ____

Main crossroads of job location ____

Square feet of home ____ Number and ages of children/seniors to be cared for ____

☐ Regular basis ☐ Temporary basis ☐ Live-out ☐ Live-in

If live-in, what living quarters are provided ____

Services needed:

☐ Housekeeper ☐ Senior care ☐ Couple ☐ Trained nanny ☐ Companion

☐ Party help ☐ Errands ☐ Family home day care ☐ Infant care ☐ Social secretary

☐ Child care ☐ Chauffeur ☐ Pet care ☐ Sitter ☐ Butler/valet

☐ Plant care ☐ Mother's helper ☐ Gardener ☐ Governess (certified teacher)

☐ somewhere in between

☐ water indoor plants

☐ mix or serve alcohol

☐ chauffeur's license required

☐ chauffeur adults

☐ chauffeur children

☐ run errands

☐ other ____

EMPLOYER REFERENCE REQUEST

____ has applied for employment. The applicant lists employment with you from ____ to ____ as a ____.

We would appreciate if you would answer the following questions listed below. Your promptness will assist us in completing his/her application. Thank you.

Name of Employer ____

Address ____ Street City State Zip

Nature of Business ____ Phone Number ____

Dates of Employment: From: ____ To: ____

Starting Salary ____ Ending Salary ____

Reason for leaving ____

PLEASE CHECK THE CHOICE THAT BEST DESCRIBES THE APPLICANT:

	EXCELLENT	GOOD	FAIR	UNSATISFACTORY
Quality of work				
Quantity of work				
Attitude				
Personality				
Attendance				
Health				
Emotional Stability				

If any choice was answered "FAIR" or "UNSATISFACTORY", please elaborate: ____

Any additional information: ____

Employer's Signature ____ Title ____

I authorize investigation of all statements contained on this form.

Applicant's Signature ____ Date ____

© 1989 Five Star Publications

8

Sample Forms

The following forms are included as illustrations and as reminders of the importance of having complete, consistent, and comparable records of applications, references and interviews.

FORM I-9

EMPLOYMENT ELIGIBILITY VERIFICATION (Form I-9)

1 EMPLOYEE INFORMATION AND VERIFICATION: (To be completed and signed by employee.)

Name: (Print or Type) Last	First	Middle	Birth Name
Address: Street Name and Number	City	State	ZIP Code
Date of Birth (Month/Day/Year)		Social Security Number	

I attest, under penalty of perjury, that I am (check a box):
- ☐ 1. A citizen or national of the United States.
- ☐ 2. An alien lawfully admitted for permanent residence (Alien Number A _____).
- ☐ 3. An alien authorized by the Immigration and Naturalization Service to work in the United States (Alien Number A _____ or Admission Number _____, expiration of employment authorization, if any _____).

I attest, under penalty of perjury, the documents that I have presented as evidence of identity and employment eligibility are genuine and relate to me. I am aware that federal law provides for imprisonment and/or fine for any false statements or use of false documents in connection with this certificate.

Signature	Date (Month/Day/Year)

PREPARER/TRANSLATOR CERTIFICATION (To be completed if prepared by person other than the employee). I attest, under penalty of perjury, that the above was prepared by me at the request of the named individual and is based on all information of which I have any knowledge.

Signature	Name (Print or Type)		
Address (Street Name and Number)	City	State	Zip Code

2 EMPLOYER REVIEW AND VERIFICATION: (To be completed and signed by employer.)

Instructions:
Examine one document from List A and check the appropriate box. *OR* examine one document from List B *and* one from List C and check the appropriate boxes. Provide the *Document Identification Number* and *Expiration Date* for the document checked.

List A Documents that Establish Identity and Employment Eligibility	List B Documents that Establish Identity	List C Documents that Establish Employment Eligibility
☐ 1. United States Passport ☐ 2. Certificate of United States Citizenship ☐ 3. Certificate of Naturalization ☐ 4. Unexpired foreign passport with attached Employment Authorization ☐ 5. Alien Registration Card with photograph	☐ 1. A State-issued driver's license or a State-issued I.D. card with a photograph, or information, including name, sex, date of birth, height, weight, and color of eyes. (Specify State)_____ ☐ 2. U.S. Military Card ☐ 3. Other (Specify document and issuing authority)_____	☐ 1. Original Social Security Number Card (other than a card stating it is not valid for employment) ☐ 2. A birth certificate issued by State, county, or municipal authority bearing a seal or other certification ☐ 3. Unexpired INS Employment Authorization Specify form # _____
Document Identification # _____ *Expiration Date (if any)* _____	*Document Identification* # _____ *Expiration Date (if any)* _____	*Document Identification* # _____ *Expiration Date (if any)* _____

CERTIFICATION: I attest, under penalty of perjury, that I have examined the documents presented by the above individual, that they appear to be genuine and to relate to the individual named, and that the individual, to the best of my knowledge, is eligible to work in the United States.

Signature	Name (Print or Type)	Title
Employer Name	Address	Date

Form I-9 (05/07/87)
OMB No. 1115-0136

U.S. Department of Justice
Immigration and Naturalization Service

EMPLOYMENT ELIGIBILITY VERIFICATION (Form I-9)

1 EMPLOYEE INFORMATION AND VERIFICATION: (To be completed and signed by employee.)

Name: (Print or Type) Last	First	Middle	Birth Name
Address: Street Name and Number	City	State	ZIP Code
Date of Birth (Month/Day/Year) 6-22-60		Social Security Number 555-66-7777	

I attest, under penalty of perjury, that I am (check a box):

- [X] 1. A citizen or national of the United States.
- [ ] 2. An alien lawfully admitted for permanent residence (Alien Number A _____).
- [ ] 3. An alien authorized by the Immigration and Naturalization Service to work in the United States (Alien Number A _____, or Admission Number _____, expiration of employment authorization, if any _____).

I attest, under penalty of perjury, the documents that I have presented as evidence of identity and employment eligibility are genuine and relate to me. I am aware that federal law provides for imprisonment and/or fine for any false statements or use of false documents in connection with this certificate.

Signature	Date (Month/Day/Year)

PREPARER/TRANSLATOR CERTIFICATION (To be completed if prepared by person other than the employee). I attest, under penalty of perjury, that the above was prepared by me at the request of the named individual and is based on all information of which I have any knowledge.

Signature	Name (Print or Type)
Address (Street Name and Number)	City	State	Zip Code

2 EMPLOYER REVIEW AND VERIFICATION: (To be completed and signed by employer.)

Instructions:
Examine one document from List A and check the appropriate box. _OR_ examine one document from List B _and_ one from List C and check the appropriate boxes. Provide the *Document Identification Number* and *Expiration Date* for the document checked.

List A Documents that Establish Identity and Employment Eligibility	List B Documents that Establish Identity	List C Documents that Establish Employment Eligibility
[ ] 1. United States Passport	[X] 1. A State-issued driver's license or a State-issued I.D. card with a photograph, or information, including name, sex, date of birth, height, weight, and color of eyes. (Specify State) **ARIZONA**	[X] 1. Original Social Security Number Card (other than a card stating it is not valid for employment)
[ ] 2. Certificate of United States Citizenship	[ ] 2. U.S. Military Card	[ ] 2. A birth certificate issued by State, county, or municipal authority bearing a seal or other certification
[ ] 3. Certificate of Naturalization	[ ] 3. Other (Specify document and issuing authority)	[ ] 3. Unexpired INS Employment Authorization Specify form # _____
[ ] 4. Unexpired foreign passport with attached Employment Authorization		
[ ] 5. Alien Registration Card with photograph		
Document Identification # _____	*Document Identification* # L34511	*Document Identification* # 555-66-7777
Expiration Date (if any)	*Expiration Date (if any)* 6-89	*Expiration Date (if any)*

CERTIFICATION: I attest, under penalty of perjury, that I have examined the documents presented by the above individual, that they appear to be genuine and to relate to the individual named, and that the individual, to the best of my knowledge, is eligible to work in the United States.

Signature	Name (Print or Type)	Title
Employer Name	Address	Date

Form I-9 (05/07/87)
OMB No. 1115-0136

U.S. Department of Justice
Immigration and Naturalization Service

JOB DESCRIPTION FORM

JOB DESCRIPTION FORM

Title of job _____
Main crossroads of job location _____
Square feet of home _____ Number and ages of children/seniors to be cared for _____
☐ Regular basis ☐ Temporary basis ☐ Live-out ☐ Live-in
If live-in, what living quarters are provided _____
Services needed:

☐ Housekeeper   ☐ Senior care   ☐ Couple   ☐ Trained nanny   ☐ Companion
☐ Party help   ☐ Errands   ☐ Family home day care ☐ Infant care   ☐ Social secretary
☐ Child care   ☐ Chauffeur   ☐ Pet care   ☐ Sitter   ☐ Butler/valet
☐ Plant care   ☐ Mother's helper   ☐ Gardener   ☐ Governess (certified teacher)
☐ Other

Job description _____
_____

Days and hours someone is needed _____ Days off _____
Salary range _____ Date for employment to begin _____
Driver needed? _____ If yes, does person need own car on the job? _____ If so, how much per mile? _____
Nearest bus route _____
Pets in home? _____ If yes, how many and what kind _____
Non-smoker preferred? _____ Does anyone in home smoke? _____
Swimming pool? _____ If yes, is a swimmer required? _____
Training required: ☐ CPR   ☐ First Aid   ☐ Life saving
Qualities look for: ☐ reserved   ☐ outgoing
I want someone who is going to be: ☐ part of family ☐ strictly an employee ☐ somewhere in between
If meals are to be prepared, employee is to: ☐ eat with family ☐ eat separately
Four most important qualifications I look for in employee
1. _____   2. _____
3. _____   4. _____
My three top reasons for not hiring someone
1. _____
2. _____
3. _____

Job requirements. Check all that apply.

☐ clean bathrooms   ☐ clean arcadia doors   ☐ prepare breakfast   ☐ water indoor plants
☐ clean French doors   ☐ do laundry   ☐ prepare lunch   ☐ mix or serve alcohol
☐ clean kitchen   ☐ iron   ☐ prepare dinner   ☐ chauffeur's license required
☐ dust   ☐ care for infant   ☐ do gourmet cooking   ☐ chauffeur adults
☐ vacuum   ☐ care for child   ☐ feed pets   ☐ chauffeur children
☐ wash dishes   ☐ change diapers   ☐ do yard work   ☐ run errands
☐ wax floors   ☐ grocery shopping   ☐ do pool work   ☐ other _____

Benefits offered
- [ ] one week paid vacation after _____ months employment.
- [ ] two weeks paid vacation after _____ months employment.
- [ ] legal holidays off with pay
- [ ] sick leave   number of sick days per month/year
- [ ] medical insurance   [ ] dental insurance   [ ] other _____

Salary evaluation
- [ ] 3 months   [ ] 6 months   [ ] 1 year   [ ] other _____

Starting salary $ _____

Comments _____
_____
_____
_____
_____
_____
_____
_____
_____
_____
_____

INTERVIEWS

Date   Person interviewed   Comments
_____
_____
_____
_____
_____
_____
_____
_____

Person selected _____
Date to start _____
Starting salary _____

© 1989 Five Star Publications

APPLICATION FOR EMPLOYMENT

APPLICATION FOR HOUSEHOLD EMPLOYMENT

We are an equal opportunity employer, dedicated to a policy of non-discrimination in hiring on any basis, including race, creed, color, age, sex, religion or national origin.

PERSONAL INFORMATION   PLEASE PRINT!   DATE _____

Full Name _____ Social Security Number _____

Address _____ How Long? _____

Previous Address _____ How Long? _____

Phone Number: Home _____   Work _____   Message _____

Are you a U.S. citizen? _____   If no, are you eligible to be employed under a visa permit? _____

State age if under 18 or over 70 : _____   Marital Status _____   Number & ages of dependents: _____

Are you a smoker? _____   Swimmer? _____   Are you certified in: ☐ CPR   ☐ First Aid   ☐ Life Saving

Is your certification current? _____   Date of expiration: _____

Transportation Available: _____   Do you have a chauffeur's license? _____

Have you ever been bonded? _____   If yes, what job(s)? _____

Have you ever been denied bond coverage? _____   If yes, please explain: _____

Have you ever entered a plea of guilty or been convicted of any crime or any moving traffic violations? _____

If yes, please explain: _____

How long have you lived in this state? _____   How did you hear about this job? _____

Please list other position(s) you are applying for: 1. _____

2. _____   3. _____

If you are applying for child care, what age(s) do you prefer to work with? _____

Will you work for a family with pets? _____

Please check your availability (check all that apply)   Full-time ☐   Part-time ☐   (list hours) _____

Live-in ☐   Live-out ☐   Temporary assignments ☐   Relocate out-of-state ☐

Other _____   Rate of pay expected: _____

EDUCATIONAL BACKGROUND

	Circle last year completed	Year graduated	Name and location of school
Elementary School	5 6 7 8		
High School	1 2 3 4		
College	1 2 3 4		
Vocational School	1 2 ___ mos.		

Foreign languages you speak, read or write well: _____

PHYSICAL RECORD

Do you have any conditions which might limit your ability to perform the job applied for? _____

If yes, please explain _____

DRIVER'S LICENSE

Do you possess a valid driver's license? _____   If yes, state issued _____   D.L. # _____

Name as it appears on the license _____   Expiration date _____

How far do you live from this job site?   ☐ less than a mile   ☐ 1-2 miles   ☐ 2-4 miles   ☐ 5 miles
                                          ☐ 6-10 miles   ☐ 10 miles or more

100

EMPLOYMENT HISTORY

List below all past employment, beginning with the most recent. Use separate sheet of paper if necessary.

Name of employer _____ Supervisor's name _____
Address _____ City, State, Zip _____
Phone number: Home _____ Office _____
Employed from _____ to _____ If child care, number of children and ages _____
If housecleaning, number of square feet _____ Days and hours worked _____
Job description _____
Reason for leaving _____ Ending salary _____

Name of employer _____ Supervisor's name _____
Address _____ City, State, Zip _____
Phone number: Home _____ Office _____
Employed from _____ to _____ If child care, number of children and ages _____
If housecleaning, number of square feet _____ Days and hours worked _____
Job description _____
Reason for leaving _____ Ending salary _____

Name of employer _____ Supervisor's name _____
Address _____ City, State, Zip _____
Phone number: Home _____ Office _____
Employed from _____ to _____ If child care, number of children and ages _____
If housecleaning, number of square feet _____ Days and hours worked _____
Job description _____
Reason for leaving _____ Ending salary _____

May we contact the employers listed above? _____ If not, which one(s) do you not wish us to contact? _____

CHARACTER REFERENCES

List below the names of two people not related to you, whom you have known at least one year:

Name & Address   Name & Address

_____   _____
_____   _____
_____   _____

Phone _____ Years known _____   Phone _____ Years known _____

The facts in my application are true and complete. You are hereby authroized to make any investigations of my personal history and financial and credit status through any credit agencies of your choice. I understand that any misrepresentation or omission of facts is cause for termination of employment. Further, I understand and agree that any employment gained is for no definite period of time and may, regardless of the date of payment of my wages and salary, be terminated at any time without any previous notice.

Signature _____ Date _____

IN ORDER TO PROCESS YOUR APPLICATION, ALL INFORMATION MUST BE COMPLETE!

© 1989 Five Star Publications

INTERVIEW IMPRESSION SHEET

INTERVIEW IMPRESSION SHEET

Candidate's Name _____ Date _____

Postion Applying For _____

AREAS OF IMPRESSION	COMMENTS
1. Appropriate Appearance	
2. Prior Work Experience	
3. Prior Job Stability	
4. Enthusiasm/Motivation	
5. Maturity/Poise	
6. Career Goals	
7. Appropriate Ability	
8. Overall Strengths	
9. Overall Weaknesses	

Additional Comments _____
_____
_____

© 1989 Five Star Publications

INTERVIEW IMPRESSION SHEET

Candidate's Name: ██████████ Date: ██████████

Postion Applying For: House Manager/Social Secretary

AREAS OF IMPRESSION	COMMENTS
1. Appropriate Appearance	Very neat, professional appearance
2. Prior Work Experience	Nurse/Teacher/Supervisor
3. Prior Job Stability	Basically stable, last two jobs were held for one year each and the one before for six years
4. Enthusiasm/Motivation	Very enthusiastic, seems highly motivated
5. Maturity/Poise	Very mature/well poised
6. Career Goals	To obtain an administrative position
7. Appropriate Ability	Seems very capable
8. Overall Strengths	Communicating
9. Overall Weaknesses	Could not think of any

Additional Comments: She has done extensive traveling in 49 states and in eight countries. Loves to travel and since her children are grown she would be free to travel as the position she is applying calls for.

© 1989 Five Star Publications

EMPLOYER REFERENCE REQUEST

EMPLOYER REFERENCE REQUEST

_____ has applied for employment.   The applicant lists employment with you from _____ to _____ as a _____.

We would appreciate if you would answer the following questions listed below.   Your promptness will assist us in completing his/her application.   Thank you.

Name of Employer _____

Address _____
              Street   City   State   Zip

Nature of Business _____ Phone Number _____

Dates of Employment: From: _____ To: _____

Starting Salary _____ Ending Salary _____

Reason for leaving _____

PLEASE CHECK THE CHOICE THAT BEST DESCRIBES THE APPLICANT:

	EXCELLENT	GOOD	FAIR	UNSATISFACTORY
Quality of work				
Quantity of work				
Attitude				
Personality				
Attendance				
Health				
Emotional Stability				

If any choice was answered "FAIR" or "UNSATISFACTORY", please elaborate: _____
_____
_____
_____

Any additional information: _____
_____
_____

Employer's Signature _____ Title _____

I authorize investigation of all statements contained on this form.

Applicant's Signature _____ Date _____

© 1989 Five Star Publications

EMPLOYER REFERENCE REQUEST

_____ has applied for employment. The applicant lists employment with you from _____ to _____ as a **Crewperson**.

We would appreciate if you would answer the following questions listed below. Your promptness will assist us in completing his/her application. Thank you.

Name of Employer: _____
Address: _____
    Street   City   State   Zip
Nature of Business: **Fast Food**   Phone Number: _____
Dates of Employment: From: **6-79** To: **8-81**
Starting Salary: **Unknown**   Ending Salary: **Unknown**
Reason for leaving: **Unknown**

PLEASE CHECK THE CHOICE THAT BEST DESCRIBES THE APPLICANT:

	EXCELLENT	GOOD	FAIR	UNSATISFACTORY
Quality of work		✓		
Quantity of work		✓		
Attitude			✓	
Personality		✓		
Attendance		✓		
Health	✓			
Emotional Stability			✓	

If any choice was answered "FAIR" or "UNSATISFACTORY", please elaborate: _____ **was a good worker, but at the time of her employment here had a bad temper. She'd become upset with something or someone, and hold a grudge all day.**

Any additional information: **I acquired this information about ____ from the manager from when she was employed here.**

Employer's Signature: _____ Title: **Store Mgr.**

I authorize investigation of all statements contained on this form.

Applicant's Signature: _____ Date: _____

© 1989 Five Star Publications

CHARACTER REFERENCE REQUEST

CHARACTER REFERENCE REQUEST

_____has applied for employment. The applicant lists you as a character reference.

We would appreciate if you would answer the following questions listed below. Your promptness will assist us in completing his/her application. Thank you.

Name of Reference _____

Address_____
          Street   City   State   Zip

Phone Number _____ Relationship_____

How long have you been acquainted with the applicant? _____

PLEASE CHECK THE CHOICE THAT BEST DESCRIBES THE APPLICANT:

	ALWAYS	USUALLY	OCCASIONALLY	NEVER
Dependable				
Trustworthy				
Honest				
Good Attitude				
Emotionally Stable				
Easy to get along with				

If any choice was answered "USUALLY", "OCCASIONALLY" or "NEVER", please elaborate: _____
_____
_____
_____

Do you highly recommend this individual for employment? _____

If no, please explain: _____
_____

Any additional information: _____
_____
_____

Reference's Signature _____

I authorize investigation of all statements contained on this form.

Applicant's Signature_____ Date _____

© 1989 Five Star Publications

CHARACTER REFERENCE REQUEST

_____ has applied for employment. The applicant lists you as a character reference.

We would appreciate if you would answer the following questions listed below. Your promptness will assist us in completing his/her application. Thank you.

Name of Reference: _____

Address: _____
Street   City   State   Zip

Phone Number: _____ Relationship: _friend_

How long have you been acquainted with the applicant? _27 years_

PLEASE CHECK THE CHOICE THAT BEST DESCRIBES THE APPLICANT:

	ALWAYS	USUALLY	OCCASIONALLY	NEVER
Dependable	x			
Trustworthy	x			
Honest	x			
Good Attitude	x			
Emotionally Stable	xx			
Easy to get along with	xxx			

If any choice was answered "USUALLY", "OCCASIONALLY" or "NEVER", please elaborate: _____

Do you highly recommend this individual for employment? _yes_

If no, please explain: _____

Any additional information: _____ is a very unusual woman, of keen intelligence, searching mind, tremendous curiousity and drive, and many professional skills and varied experience She is a gifted landscape architect, a dedicated teacher and capable of executing any kind of project she undertakes.

Reference's Signature: _____

I authorize investigation of all statements contained on this form.

Applicant's Signature: _____ Date: _____

© 1989 Five Star Publications

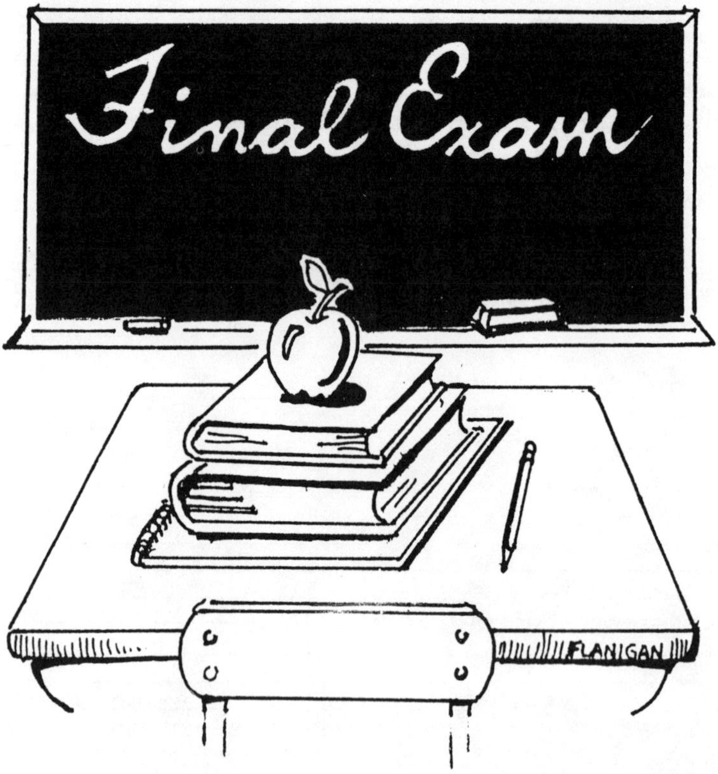
Final Exam
FLANIGAN

EPILOGUE

The Test

I know the temptation is great to just skip to this test. But I believe you need to read this book first. Go back, read the book and then take the test.

Nannies, Maids & More

1. You're interviewing for a sitter. Two don't show, one is late, and the one who shows up has no teeth and great references. **Should you:**

    a. Hire "No teeth" and keep lots of baby food in the house.

    b. Keep another ad running at $25.00 an ad and keep those late night calls coming in.

    c. Enroll in a nanny school and become a qualified nanny and take the job yourself.

2. You've just hired the greatest live-in housekeeper and she just informed you that her mother and father are moving in with her. **You:**

    a. Say welcome "Mom" and "Dad", make yourself at home.

    b. Suddenly come up with the urge to clean your own 6,000-square-foot home.

    c. Inform your husband that he is going to clean your 6,000-square-foot home.

    d. Sell the estate and buy a two-bedroom mobile home.

    You have already tried b. and c., so the only correct choice is d.

3. It's time for work and your sitter is late (again). **What do you do:**

    a. Call in sick again. *(You really didn't want to go to work anyway)*

    b. Call a friend's sitter and see if you can lure her away, *(those freshly baked brownies will lure anyone. If those brownies don't work, try cheese cake.)*

    c. Quit your job, stay home permanently with your little darlings. *(Who wanted a second car, and those high mortgage payments anyway?)*

The Test

4. Your sitter has called you at work, you are in a meeting negotiating a million-dollar contract. She needs to talk to you now. **You tell your secretary to:**

    a. Go away
    b. Handle it anyway she wants to
    c. Set up an appointment
    d. Consult with the gardener and the maid, and whatever they agree on is fine.

5. Your fifth sitter in the past five months has informed you she is pregnant, **what now?**

    a. Tell her you'll add a wing to your home, hire a nanny for her.
    b. Fire her and have her collect unemployment insurance.
    c. Give her a baby shower at your earliest convenience.

    I know the choice is a tough one but there are two right answers in this category. First you give her a baby shower, then contact your builder and have a wing added on. You know how hard it was to find her. Let this one get away and you may not have a decent sitter for months.

6. You have been interviewing for a month for a senior care provider for your parents, after putting $150.00 into ads, and having a zillion no shows, and those that did show, are not your cup of tea, **you decided to:**

    a. Call an agency and pay them any amount to find someone for you.
    b. See a.
    c. See b.
    d. All of the above.

    We had to give you an easy one. For those of you who missed this one, you need to read the book all over again.

All kidding aside the task of hiring is not an easy one. Speaking as a former agency owner. I found it was much easier to sign up clients who had searched on their own. (And probably more than once.)

It made our job easier and one that was accompanied by lots of praise, hugs, and many times the promise of cheesecake.

If you would like to share some of your hiring experiences, write to me c/o Five Star Publications, P.O. Box 3142 Scottsdale, AZ 85271-3142. Some of your experiences might be used in future publications.

Linda F. Radke

OTHER FIVE STAR PUBLICATIONS

OPTIONS: A Directory of Child & Senior Services
The Options Directory covers the Phoenix, Tucson, Flagstaff and Yuma areas in Arizona. Nearly 300 services listed. Each listing includes description of service, phone number, address, licensing status, owner or director and year of establishment.

"I personally feel this material would be of great value...to assist employees who have child or adult care responsibilities. Let's face it – the two-worker family is here to stay and many absences from work are associated with child or parent care problems. OPTIONS is the only directory I have seen which puts so much (of this) type of information under one cover."

Robert L. Scott, Jr., President
Arizona Employer's Council, Inc.

(Watch for our 1989 edition, which will feature a national listing of nanny schools and placement agencies.)

Shakespeare for Children: The Story of Romeo & Juliet.
Author Cass Foster is an Assistant Professor of Theater at Ohio State University at Mansfield. Foster magically blended Shakespeare's verse with narration and illustrations by Sandy Boggs, to challenge, mystify and delight those who desire a fuller appreciation of the works of Shakespeare. The easy-to-read pages will intill confidence in parents, teachers and young children as they explore the beauty and splendor of one of Shakespeare's greatest masterpieces, Romeo & Juliet.

"The selections of passages were excellent and very clear...you've got a hit on your hands."

Lynn Dominick, Head Librarian
Galion Public Library, Galion, Ohio

ORDER FORM

Five Star Publications

P.O. Box 3142
Scottsdale, AZ 85271-3142
Telephone (602) 941-0770

Please send me the following books published through Five Star Publications:

_____	copies of **Nannies, Maids & More**	$14.95 ea.
_____	copies of **OPTIONS: A Directory of Child & Senior Services**	$9.95 ea.
_____	copies of **Shakespeare for Children: The Story of Romeo & Juliet** (available summer of 1989)	$14.95 ea.

Inquire about volume discounts.

Name _____

Address _____

City _____ State _____ Zip _____

Phone _____

Arizonans please add 6.5% sales tax.

Shipping - $1.50 for the first book/$.75 for each additional book.

_____ I want my publication(s) shipped Air Mail. I have included an additional $3.00 for Air Mail.

_____ Please add my name to your mailing list

THANK YOU FOR YOUR ORDER

FORMS AVAILABLE THROUGH FIVE STAR PUBLICATIONS

Five Star Publications
P.O. Box 3142
Scottsdale, AZ 85271-3142
Telephone (602) 941-0770

*As shown in **Nannies, Maids & More***

ORDER FORM

Name _____

Company _____

Address _____

City _____ State _____ Zip _____

Phone _____

FORMS NEEDED (50 per pkg.)	Cost	# of packs	Total
Household Employment Application	$14.95	_____	_____
Interview Impression Form	$14.95	_____	_____
Employer Reference Form	$14.95	_____	_____
Character Reference Form	$14.95	_____	_____
SHIPPING & HANDLING			
1 – 5 packages	$1.50		_____
5 – 10 packages	$3.00		_____
10 or more	$ .30 per pkg		_____
TOTAL ENCLOSED			

Arizonans please add 6.5% sales tax.
Please make checks payable to Five Star Publications.

I would like to charge my order. Charge to my ☐ MC ☐ Visa

Card # _____ Expiration Date _____

Print name exactly as on card _____

Signature _____

All forms are non-refundable once ordered.

_____ I want my forms Air Mailed. I have enclosed $3.00 additional.

_____ Please add my name to your mailing list.

THANK YOU FOR YOUR ORDER